# SELF-CARE ANGEL MAGIC BEGINS NOW

VEENU SANDHU

To the Divine

To the Generational Blessings

To my grandfather, Late S. Lal Singh (a freedom fighter)

To Papa S. Ajit Singh and Maa Ms. Karminder Kaur

For choosing me as the conduit to pass on the legacy of writing

# Contents

# Contents

# Foreword

Life is a puzzle, and guess the weird part? We all think that we know how to solve it. Why not? We have frameworks and we believe in copy-pasting the tried and tested methods of living life, which are: Study, Salary, Spouse, Safety, and Kids, and the cycle repeats.

What we never think about is THE COST. Sleepless nights? Oh, part and parcel. Anxiety? Oh, what's life without it, right? Skipped meal? A medal for many? We limp, we sleepwalk, and yet, we pretend that autopilot is the best way to land in our wonderlands. Result? The wonderland often leaves us wondering whether this was really worth being called a wonderland.

What do we rarely realise? That burnout is just the symptom. Self-abandonment is the root cause.

Veenu's book is not a traditional guide. It doesn't shout instructions. It holds your hand. It pauses with you. And then, like a wise elder or a kind friend, it gently nudges you to wake up, to stretch into your own skin again.

As a book writing coach, I often tell writers that their real story begins where their resistance ends. And the author of this book didn't just end resistance; she wrestled with it, danced with it, and then wrote about it with disarming vulnerability.

This isn't just a book about health. It's about healing. Not the curated kind you find on spa brochures, but the raw, ragged, breathtaking kind that begins when you finally pause and ask, "What about me?"

So, if you're holding this book while multitasking, nursing burnout, or looking for some lost version of yourself, breathe. This book doesn't ask you to change your life overnight. It simply reminds you that you are worth showing up for every single day.

Because stories don't just heal readers, they rescue the writer first.

Heena M ShrivastavaAuthor-5 booksInternational Book Writing CoachFounder- WriternaamaICF-PCC, Certified NLP Trainer

# Preface

Everyone born on this earth is destined to face life's challenges, although their types and intensity vary from individual to individual. Life ensures that no one is spared from struggles uniquely crafted for them. These trials pull us underwater, not to drown us, but to cleanse us of our vices and help us discover our true worth.

What makes this book unique is that it is born from my real imperfections, personal challenges, tested methods, and honest healing journey, all rooted in Self-Care. Your experiences, voids, or wounds may differ from mine, perhaps even more profound, but the practical solutions offered here are grounded in clarity, logic, and an understanding of the root causes. With consistent practice, these approaches become easier and sustainable.

You will likely resonate with many of the stories in this book. They aren't just experiences, they're roadmaps. You'll find tools that can be moulded to fit your needs, making healing and balance possible.

Just as they say, "Need is the mother of invention", my need was simple: to find a way to be happy like a child, every time. This deep yearning led me to a Law of Attraction course in 2015, Meditation in 2020, and the realisation that I had been living trapped in self-doubt, limiting beliefs, and emotional resistance. What I was really searching for was Self-Care.

To deepen this path, I was fortunate to meet Ms. Harpreet Kaur in 2021, who introduced me to healing modalities that reshaped me from the inside out. In 2023, I became a certified Yoga Trainer through Bodhi School of Yoga, Hyderabad, another milestone in balancing my emotional, physical, and mental health.

Through Self-Care's holistic power, I reinvented myself as a more confident, peaceful, and present Veenu. This transformation led me to Heena M. Srivastava, a compassionate national-international book coach, who encouraged me to bring this book to life, so that others, too, may find their own healing through Self-Care.

As much as I poured love, insight, and lived wisdom into this book, I truly believe you'll receive the same in return. Remember, Self-Care is a journey, not a destination.

If you seek happiness, calm, and emotional strength, at any time, any place, at any age, this book is your disguised blessing.

I would love to hear your reflections and the benefits you experienced. Write to me at: Sveenu146@gmail.comOr DM me on Instagram: @veenu_sandhu

With heartfelt warmth, Veenu Sandhu

# Acknowledgements

I offer the deepest gratitude, with unending thanks to the Divine, for allowing me to write this book and fulfil its dream of spreading the wisdom of Self-care in the world.

I offer my heartfelt gratitude to the lineage of writing that was passed down to me through my father and late Freedom Fighter Grandfather, who used to write poems.

Also endless thanks to my always supportive parents for infusing positive energy and courage into their eldest average child (that's me) amongst their three other younger genius children, unconditionally loving me even when I did blunders and instilling confidence to help me to break old limiting parameters of achievements which eventually fruitified into this book.

With deep gratitude, I thank the people who sensed this part of me and sowed the seed in my mind by advising me at different times to write a book, which I initially ridiculed in utter disbelief. Yet, my subconscious mind brought it to light with this book.

Huge thanks to my mentors, Ms. Neeru Mahajan, Ms. Harpreet Kaur, and Ms. Tapaswinee Hota Choudhary, who arrived in my life at the right time to illuminate my path with magnificent support by sharing their Vast wisdom, compassion, divinity, and encouraging teachings, loaded with meditations to uplift me and fly beyond.

No word is suffice to express my inner gratitude to 5 AM Club (founder-Mr. Pranav Patil) through whom I met co-member of 5 AM club Ms. Heena M Shrivastava (esteemed author of 4 books and Book Coach of many reputed authors) who with her divinity, inner purity, intelligence, writing skills, updated techniques and experience of mentoring skills, litburning fire within me to write a book and her inspiring assistance with holistic approach from ideating chapters to designing the cover page brought forth this book magically.

My sincere thanks to Bodhi School of Yoga, Hyderabad, for imparting the invaluable teachings of Yoga and Health and Wellness Coaching, whose impact on the transformation of my life encouraged me to share the importance of Yoga in Self Care through this Book.

Thanks to my husband for giving me the space and freedom to write about my life experiences in this book. A Big thanks with enormous gratitude to my loving sons, Arshdeep Singh and Harkirat Singh, for always encouraging me wholeheartedly with their constructive support from overseas, especially on the technical front, and cheering for my achievements.

Thanks to my precious three Siblings, extended families, and well-wishers from all quarters of the small world around for their true love, prayers, and blessings worked as a life force to create this book.

My thank-you offerings would be incomplete without mentioning the very special three co-travellers (Dimple, Shweta, and Prasanna) on my deeper spiritual journey for having unwavering faith (more than me ) since the year 2021 that sooner or later I would write a book, which amazingly brought this book into your hands.

A special thanks to my house help and her studious daughter, Khushi for taking care of my household chores and providing me a peaceful environment and sufficient time to scribe this book.

Last but not least, massive thanks with sincere wishes to publishers, editors and readers of my first literary work who have chosen and picked up this book that mentioned tools and techniques of Self Care bring a paradigm shift in your precious lives as you all are God's child and deserve a happy life.

# Introduction

SELF-CARE IS AN INVESTMENT IN THE BANK CALLED
"YOUR WELL-BEING".
ARE YOU INVESTING REGULARLY?

Once, a loving king felt his left eye turn red. Still, he didn't bother and kept himself busy for the betterment of his kingdom so that everyone in his kingdom lived happily. After a few days, his right eye also started to become red and heavy. Still, he didn't tell anyone and continued to work diligently for his kingdom. Then, one day, he felt unbearable pain in both eyes and found it difficult even to open his eyes. Many doctors worldwide were consulted, and the entire city was now alarmed. Nothing worked. No one could bring him the respite now.

Coincidentally, after a few days, one intelligent Sage visited the King's kingdom. He claimed that he could save the King's eyes. He was summoned to the court immediately. "The more green you see, the faster your eyes recover. Everyone in the court was astonished to get such a simple solution for the King. Nevertheless, the King wanted to give it a shot.

After some days, the Sage returned to meet the King, surprised to see the whole city painted green. Everyone he met in the town criticised the King's decision and was unhappy. When he met the King to enquire about his eyes, the King thanked him and said his idea worked like magic. His eyes were cured, but he was also sad, as the villagers found this change uncomfortable.

Then he told King, "I am delighted to see your eyes getting cured, my great King. But why so much effort to paint everything green? Couldn't My Majesty have just worn a green goggle?"

*Do you find yourself in the shoes of that King?*

Who is more bothered about others' happiness and well-being?

Who doesn't keep his/her health and happiness above everything and everyone?

Who, instead of attending to himself/herself first on time to be happy and healthy, wants everyone and every situation around him/her, including time, to favour him/her to be happy?

Who wants everyone to listen to his/ her advice without listening to their own mind and body?

If you answered YES, then consider this a wake-up call. This book is made for you.

Self-care is giving your mind-body-heart unconditional love when they feel alone and need a helping hand to heal them.

# Chapter 1: Self-Care Simplified

**What do you think self-care is?**

- Is it indulging in massages/pedicures/retreats?
- Is it buying costly cosmetic products?
- Is it sharing your filtered pics on social media and receiving fake appreciation?
- Need Luxurious time to do this?
- Is it ignoring family /professional responsibilities?

My understanding of self-care was similar to how a 3-year-old would describe taxation. (It may be just a spelling for them, or who cares?)

Self-care was introduced to me through reels and short videos, as well as full-length videos that guided users on enjoying spa treatments, buying trendy clothes, going on vacations, posting beautiful pictures, and collecting appreciation. I panicked because my self-care mark sheet was a zero in this sphere.

Nevertheless, I vowed to enter the University of Whatsapp, YouTube, and super addictive and exhausting scrolls, and I sat with pen and paper. Like a diligent student,

I took notes and made a never-ending list of (primarily non-doable) practices, leaving me only with burnout, jealousy, and inferiority.

Fancy ads on social sites were screaming for my time and money, as if not spending any of these would put me in hell. Self-care suddenly seemed like the most challenging exam of my life—not made for the ignorant one like me, who had a longer list of responsibilities and other tasks on my plate.

After doing my PhD in reels, Instagram, and YouTube shorts, I came to my verdict:

This Self-care would not put food on the table or pay the family's bills.

So, self-care is just another trend on social media, and I was waiting for this storm to settle.

Then came the defining year of our lives: COVID-19, which redefined many things, including self-care.

"March 2021 turned out to be the darkest month for my health. Corona hijacked my already sulking health and immune system. My not-so-good eating habits and lack of exercise (in the name of 'no time') added fuel to the fire of my already plummeting health. My intestine went almost on a ventilator, resulting in acute pain, and toppled up my bowel system. My taste buds went on strike, and I could no longer detect the taste of salt. From eating mindlessly, I reached a stage where my mind stopped me from eating.

A month passed, and I had to return to my office work, as medicines had become my primary diet.

Office work took a further toll on my health. It was as if medicines were also giving up on me. The hospital became my second home, and doctors became my first family, who would always send me back with more medicines and more sermons on having patience. In ancient times, during the

Treta Yuga, the Gods incarnated whenever the Earth was burdened with injustice. In this Kalyuga, the Gods have delegated tasks to algorithms, and those algorithms show us the exact things we are going through in life. So, it was my time for the algorithm to read my mind and follow the commands of the Almighty.

While scrolling, a video popped up on my screen, and my curiosity got the better of me. "Although Covid has turned out to be the biggest enemy of the human race, few superhumans have ridden the ride so well that the pandemic was scared to touch them." The narrator on the screen spoke with dragon-sized vigour and electric animation in gestures as if he had dug out the secret from the civilisations.

"Not another weirdo trick, please." I rolled my eyes and kept my fingers crossed. At that time, everyone had become a doctor on social media, and my mind was stuck in the cobwebs of unrealistic, untested, and unverified solutions.

"Before you think that this video is another crappy one where the narrator is just trying to make money online through views or is just happy that he is still employed through this fun thing, brace yourself. I would suggest you immediately toss the phone aside and never touch it to watch these crappy videos only after listening to the next line." This was weird. So all he wanted to do was to make me listen to the following line and get it done with? I was glued to the screen, and my ears were alert.

"The research shows that people who have surpassed COVID have just one superpower." The pause he took after it was itching me as if the candy was hanging next to my mouth, and I was waiting for it to land on my tongue.

"The superpower is known as physical activity. Yes! Don't believe it? As I said, toss the phone aside and kick your brain to think about the neighbourhood. Who are the ones who are still untouched by COVID?" As his words fell on my ears, my eyes popped out of my sockets, and my mind raced towards counting the folks in the neighbourhood.

Suddenly, it felt like the car I was driving had a blurry windshield, and someone had just come and cleaned it up. Be it Mrs Nalini Gupta, who still swept the floor with her mask on, or Rajkumar Joshi bhai, who was spotted daily at 6 AM on his rooftop doing yoga and pranayama, they had made it to the end of the race alive and healthy. No matter how often I ignored them because I was so busy sulking about COVID-19 and its effects, I realised they were the real heroes.

Although I don't remember the exact date, I would still call it a 'milestone day' when the war began—the battle between my growth mindset and unhelpful perceptions. Suddenly, I felt like the kidnapped Sita, for whom the war between good and evil began. I knew I had to win because my soul's essence of health was at stake.

The first change that surfaced was my focus shifting to utilising my screen time. Instead of mindlessly browsing sulking videos about COVID-19, I began searching for tips and tricks to work on myself during this period, and a flood of information emerged. Confession- for a moment, self-sabotage kicked in, and I wondered, Where was I? In what cobweb of toxicity was I browsing? Thankfully, the insight was even more potent than the self-doubt or self-rebuking.

The next phase of transformation came when I began drowning in the ocean. This vast ocean of information about self-care and maintaining health during the pandemic started to baffle me. "I am not cut out for all this. Why am I even wasting my time?" I texted one of my besties about my life to learn about the health pitfalls.

"Who is asking you to be a soldier for your health? Be the queen and hire a soldier, my lady." Her reply made me think. And before I could sulk a bit more on where to hire and whom to hire, my best friend became the fairy and sent me a contact of an online therapist.

If the pandemic was a time of doom for all, it also brought a ray of hope or a different metamorphosis for those who could remove the blindfold of self-pity and complaining. My online yoga sessions were the first stepping stones that helped me shed my perceptions of self-pity and cribbing and redirected me to the right path. It was as if I suddenly had a GPS, which showed me the easiest, smoothest, and least time-consuming path with the least traffic.

These health and wellness sessions helped me carve a new path of holistic health, where my mind, body, and soul gradually aligned with Yoga and pranayama. January 22 turned out to be the year of my rebirth. I was renewed physically, mentally, and emotionally. There was a spark in my eyes and a fire in my heart, and I was looking forward to getting up every morning.

The definition of self-care was now crystal clear to me. It was neither face packs nor spas. It was deliberate in caring for your well-being through restorative activities, which help you create healthy and functional relationships with yourself by recharging you to face any challenges with resilience. It is adequate attention to one's own physical and psychological wellness (Beauchamp and Childress, 2001)

In childhood, there was a term to foster the healthy habit of eating fruits every day: "One apple every day keeps your doctor away." The quote makes so much sense, not just literally, but also metaphorically. Apple is the self-care one needs to have every day. It may be a physical apple for a month (physical exercises), and then it can shift gears to a mental apple, where one is taking care of his/her mental health. Or it can be an emotional or spiritual one. The more consistency in eating this proverbial apple, the healthier one would be.

Now, many of us may not like apples, but love oranges. Fret not! As long as it aligns with holistic health goals, the tools you use don't matter. It is like choosing broccoli every day and experimenting with recipes to avoid boredom. As long as it is broccoli every day and serves the purpose of holistic health, nothing else matters.

During my Yoga training and health and wellness coaching at the Bodhi School of Yoga in Hyderabad, I gained a new insight into self-care being about PAUSE. "

Imagine if you were a car and were constantly on the go, breaking all traffic signals, what would happen? Chances are that you might bump into a vehicle, risking your dear life. Self-care is your speed breaker, saving you from the fatal accidents in life.We often think that sleep is enough for rest. However, how many times do we wake up feeling tired and energy-less? Ever wondered the reason?

It is because only our body is sleeping, while the mind and soul are wide awake, constantly running to chase nothing, just like those dogs that run behind cars and vehicles, not knowing what they will do once they catch up.

The focus of self-care should be on creating sustainable mechanisms that allow us to feel increased balance and pleasure in our day-to-day lives, which can be beneficial in any situation. Some of the doable activities which I keep choosing to do daily are -

**1. Simple activities –**

- Taking rest for some time in silence
- Hugging yourself lovingly
- Enjoying breathing in silence
- Smelling natural air
- Simple stroll at home in an open space {on terrace/balcony/outside home},
- Getting haircut
- Taking a break between the different tasks for at least 1 minute, breathing/muscle relaxation at the workplace
- Listening to your favourite music
- Calling a friend or someone who can make you laugh, or at least advise something positive to raise you up
- Enjoying tea in the garden/with books
- Taking good sleep
- Doing any fun activity by yourself or with children
- Doing some creative work
- Organising the cupboard
- Watching a favourite show
- Cooking a new dish of your interest, etc.

**2 Some are recurring activities and very important to follow, like –**

- Consulting counsellor
- Visiting doctor
- Meditations
- Physical activity,
- Getting in touch with your values
- Gratitude journal writing
- Reflections
- Self-counselling

- Taking online classes of your interest

**Disclaimer of Self-Care**

Self-care is not a paracetamol for all types of fevers. Different types of self-care cater to different kinds of imbalances. It may be physical issues, emotional ones, spiritual ones, or mental health issues. As the issue differs, so does the self-care.

So, here are a few things which I learnt in this journey of my self-care, and you can consider them as disclaimers for self-care:

- There is no cookie-cutter self-care. You have all the freedom to tailor it according to your surroundings, conditions, and time availability.
- As everyone is different, so are his/her requirements, so consider it as a science lab, where you experiment in test tubes and see what formation comes up and suits you the best.
- Practice is the only key to being the best version of yourself.
- Continue pursuing your passions and adding feathers to your cap that reflect your identity.
- Continue learning new things, as age is merely a measure of your evolution.

Remember the children's favourite cartoon, Doremon? He depicts the best example of self-care. How?Well, Doraemon is always looking for solutions from within. Self-care enables us to do the same. Are you ready to be your own Doraemon?

>>*Self-Care Myths*

Let's delve deeper into this table, describing the difference between what constitutes self-care and what doesn't.

| Sr.no. | Self-care is not | Self-care is |
| --- | --- | --- |
| 1. | Not just a pleasure-seeking activity | A skill to love ourselves by listening to what you and only you need to refill yourself first with positivity and health. |
| 2. | Pampering your outer body only | Aligning your mind and body to feel powerful every time |
| 3. | Fixed/perfect/right pattern/ A structured way or a checklist | An activity/practice which makes you feel better in a given/required time. |
| 4. | Is not a goal to achieve | The lifetime journey's process involves different practices as per the need in any given moment. |
| 5. | Taboo/ (because since childhood we have only learnt that, except for us, everything is an issue to attend) | Self-acknowledgement of your existence by authentically serving yourself |
| 6. | Selfish to take care of yourself | Essential process to survive with respect |
| 7. | Status symbol/fashion faux pas | The necessity to rewire the neurons on the positive pathway to be a self-support system in any real challenge. |
| 8. | Occasional activity | Consciously and continuously doing some activity for the mind, body and soul's health. |

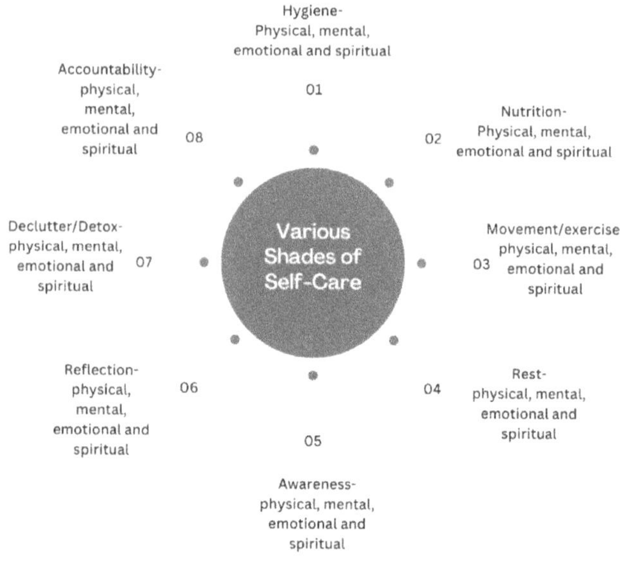


Now let's have a look at the statistics of the drastic results of not having your proverbial apples and oranges for a longer time through some research.

The World Health Organisation reports that-

- Nearly one billion people worldwide suffer from some mental disorder.
- The latest survey by India's National Institute of Mental Health and Neurosciences (NIMHANS) found that nearly 150 million Indians need mental health care services, but fewer than 30 million are seeking care.
- A study also revealed that the Mind and Body are interdependent, helping an individual behave in a proper and balanced way both inside and outside. The

mind influences the body's functioning through thoughts, feelings, and beliefs, and the Body influences the mind's functioning through body sensations.

These statistics loomed large in front of me, as if a huge tornado of cautionary warnings was swirling towards me.

Thankfully, I spotted it from a distance and kick-started my journey of self-development and self-care at the age of 45.

People may prepare to retire from work at 53, but my self-work started at 53, yet I never regretted it.

With holistic health as my ultimate goal, I obtained the following certifications as the first step in my awakening.

1. Certification (online) course of International Yoga trainer, level 1 and level 2 from Bodhi School of Yoga, Hyderabad, India, helped me to be always ready with a healthy mind and body's power of resilience in advance before any challenging moment comes.

2. Certification(online) course of Health and wellness Coach, which taught me how our lifestyle is causing imbalance inside and outside. It was an eye-opening experience for me that our denial mode of inner disturbance is life-threatening.

3. Certification course in my favourite form of dance (currently pursuing) (i.e., kathak)-after a 40-year gap since my childhood (like our yoga school says- Be the example to encourage others)

4. This book in your hands is another trophy for me, which will be stamped by your learnings and takeaways.

5. Online Yoga Training - With all this in mind and abundance raining down on me with divine grace, I began teaching yoga to different age groups.

6.  learnt Reiki healing
7.  Certification in Ashtlaxmi Reiki healing

>>Still Thinking: Why Should I Practice Self-Care?

Imagine $80,000 being credited to your balance every single day, with the condition that you must utilise this amount every day. Otherwise, by nightfall, the balance resets to zero, regardless of whether you spend it or not. The next day, you receive an additional $80,000 in your account.

In such a scenario, what would you do with the daily inflow of credit in your account?

- *Would you allow that credit to expire unused?*

>>*What if this account is known as 'Age'?*

Each day, with the sunrise, we are granted a new credit of age. Yet, if we let it pass without using it to embrace joy, happiness, health, excitement, learning, and exploring the world, we waste it under the guise of time or ageing.

Just visualise what the end will be?

>> *Who Needs Self-Care?*

- All ages: from childhood to seniors
- All genders
- All marital statuses: unmarried, married
- Urban or rural dwellers
- Working women, homemakers, or work-from-home individuals
- All professions: online, offline, big or small
- All work types: from basic to busiest
- Better parenting: for children of all ages
- Servicemen/retirees

- All societies, religions, and sects
- Anyone at any stage of health issues

In the context of Self-Care necessity, I came across a beautiful Verse from the Holy Bible on 'Our Bible Heritage '-on Google:-

*Exodus 20:8-10*

*"Remember the Sabbath day, to keep it holy. Six days you shall labor, and do all your work, but the seventh day is a Sabbath day to the Lord your God."- Exodus*

*Now, what is your take on self-care?*

One step of a winding journey toward the inside ignites

spiral of positive energy lifting you for your

highest good, but one single step to escape the

Feeling ignites the loop of your downfall.

(unknown)

# Chapter 2: Self-Care Spiral or Loop

**Self-Care Questionnaire**

i) At what time are you holding this book in your hand?

- After all household chores?
- In between rest breaks?
- In a coffee shop?
- In the lounge?
- On the passenger seat?
- Before bedtime?
- Free time?

ii) How were you feeling just before holding this book in your hand?

- Exhausted
- Buzzing
- Excited
- Happy
- Fresh
- Sleepy

**Time for meditation:**

- Take 3 deep breaths normally
- Mentally write RELAX in capital letters in front of your eyes, repeat the spelling, and say 'RELAX' 5 times mentally.
- Now inhale & exhale till you finish backwards counting from 20 to 1
- At each exhalation, keep counting back until you reach 1. For example, inhale, and while exhaling, say 20 RELAX-19, RELAX-18, RELAX-17, and so on, until 1.
- It will take hardly 3-4 sets of breathing.
- Now, slowly close your eyes, and be in this mode of stillness for a few seconds.

**How are you feeling now?**
1. Don't want to come out of this stillness
2 . Extremely Elated
3 . Infinite joy
4 . Relaxed
5. All of the above
*What do you think is the reason for this profound peace you've created in just five minutes, without any struggle?*
The reason is-

- It was a pause that your mind and body took, creating instant magic.
- Your mind and body were happily playing the game of breath in and breath out.
- The mind was focusing on numbers, and the body was breathing
- The mind forgot to wander, body sensations slowed down, the mind created happy chemicals, and the body

felt relaxed.

Make it a daily habit to engage your mind and body in a special game within your comfort zone, even if just for a few minutes. In return, they will empower you to navigate life's playground throughout the day.

Imagine you are in your favourite airline, relishing the lull in the air while the plane soars into the sky.

Despite being at an altitude of thousands of feet, you remain relaxed, but suddenly turbulence erupts, and you hear the calming sound of the crew instructing you to stay seated while buckling your seatbelt and pulling out your oxygen mask. If you notice, the crew asks you to put your mask first before helping others, and to many, it may sound selfish, right?

Self-care works on the same principle: putting your mask on first before helping others. If you have not put on your mask, how long can you help others without inhaling oxygen first?

*Still not convinced?*

Let me ask you a straightforward yet thoughtful question-

If you have taken on the responsibility of serving water to everyone, but all you have in hand is an empty vessel, how would you feed others when your vessel is not filled?

To care for others, you must first take care of yourself. If you label this as selfish, ask yourself: -

Who are you consistently putting on the back burner?

In the initial days of my inner journey to rediscover myself, I used to read motivational thoughts a lot. I came across one of the best motivational speakers, Lisa Nichols's above thought, which ignited my urge to fill myself first to create the environment around me that I favor.

**The Spiral Theory Of Self-Care**

"Anita and Vinita were not only best friends and next-door neighbours, but also shared the same workspace and family structure, each caring for two kids and elderly in-laws.

Despite having so many similarities, their happiness levels were starkly different. Vinita was a cold-natured person, often feeling lonely, and kept her emotional barriers up constantly, which became a hindrance to her ability to mingle, interact with people, and leave her mark. Vinita's to-do list never ended, and despite her work hours coming to a close, her frowns and frustrations never ceased; she carried that emotional baggage home.

Result? Disharmony in relationships leads to even more frustration for her.

Anita, on the other hand, was living life queen-size. With the same family structure, she was doing all things right. Whether it was raising emotionally resilient kids, selflessly caring for her in-laws, or nurturing an ever-blossoming relationship with her husband, Anita was proving her mettle and leaving her footprints behind. Charming everyone at the workplace was also child's play for her. "

So, what was the game changer here? What was the difference that made a difference in Anita's life?

No, it was not destiny or karma.

It was Anita's prioritising of her self-care through various rituals.

The difference could be spotted in the tiniest of ways.

The way Anita began her mornings and the way Vinita did created a stark difference in their approach towards life.

Anita's morning began with a pause, reflection, and a little breathing. She made sure to fill herself before she fed the world.

On the contrary, Vinita woke up from bed. She rushed into the kitchen as if shot out of a cannon, which sent her sympathetic system (an anxious mind) into overdrive, and, as a result, her parasympathetic system was shut down.

Anita knew when to say 'no' to others so that she could say a 'yes' to her own needs.

Anita knew when to say 'no' to others so that she could say a 'yes' to her own needs.

Vinita wanted to be in everyone's good books, a good mother, wife, daughter, daughter-in-law, and employee. In her quest to meet everyone's expectations, she failed to realise that by saying 'yes' to others, she was saying 'no' to herself, neglecting her self-care. She believed self-care was indulgent and a waste of money and time, which ultimately led to stress, anxiety, and constant fatigue.

In short, Anita was in the upward spiral of self-care, but Vinita, on the other hand, was in a loop.

**Still not convinced about self-care?**

Let's have a look at all the shades of freedom you will have in your life through self-care.

i) Short-Term

- Higher level of energy
- Increased self-worth
- Feelings of belongingness
- Increased Feeling of the beauty of life

ii) Long-Term

- Healthy mind, body, balanced emotions
- Healthy relationships
- Improved job satisfaction

- Improved quality of life

**When we don't fix self-care into our daily schedule, our body becomes a guest of -**

- Chronic mental health issues- depression, anxiety, or dementia
- Emotional blocks result in heart issues, obesity, kidney dysfunction, and insomnia
- Inner turbulences cause cancer
- Procrastination due to Low energy
- Feeling hopeless
- Urges to eat 'comfort' foods for self-smoothing
- Burnout, loud thinking
- Lack of focus
- Strained sour relationship with family and society
- No involvement with children
- Reduced performance at work and home
- Less motivation to engage in social activities
- No connection with the beauty of nature, the universe
- Regular doctor visits and skyrocketing medical treatment costs gallop through the finances.

Warning signs highlighted by researchers, which I read on Google-
i) The Deloitte study also found that 80% of India's workforce reported mental health issues.

- Fear of social stigmas around mental health issues prevented 39% of the affected respondents from taking steps to address it.
- This also affects the financial economy.

ii) The latest survey by India's National Institute of Mental Health and Neurosciences (NIMHANS) found that -

- Nearly 150 million Indians need mental health care services, but fewer than 30 million are seeking care.
- In India, mental health issues were seen, especially among white-collar workers.

iii) An article by Venkatesan Chakrapani and Shalini Bharat (2023) mentions that in a Fast-paced lifestyle and race to overtake the peers in results/ status, people are ignoring self-care through taking rest, taking pause, and overhauling the health, emotions, and mind setup, which is resulting in

- 17.7% share of the global population, India contributes significantly to the global mental health burden.
- common mental disorders (CMDs) such as depressive and anxiety disorders was 5·1% (95% CI: 5.06–5.13).
- rising divorce rates and relationship conflicts, pressure to excel at education or in the workplace.
- stress, stigma and discrimination faced by people with marginalized identities contribute to mental health problems.

All these researched facts shout an unsaid emergency, where the silence of drowning mental health is getting louder day by day.

However, research is just the tip of the iceberg. Underneath, the real problem lies in the lack of self-care. If self-care is embedded in our lifestyles, we would not witness the mental health thunderstorm.

mental health disorders are breaking out into depression, anxiety, and bipolar disorder globally.

The COVID-19 pandemic further exacerbated these challenges, leading to increased rates of mental health issues.

So, break the loop of an emotionless, robotic life of waking up, running, working, loading, stressing, and then sleeping again.

Dive into a self-care routine spiral - Inhale fresh air, a hearty smile, and carve out the best version of yourself with a healthier, happier mind and body for the precious you and for the people who need you to enrich their lives.

**"Self-care is giving the world the best of you, instead of what's left of you."** (Katie Reed)

The mind is the cave your body fears to enter; But hold the treasure you seek to live to life of your dreams.

# Chapter 3: Mind & Body Alignment

a) **"Self-care habits will shape your identity, and your identity will shape your self-care habits."**

After Virat Kohli led the team to win IPL 2024, I saw the Indian Prime Minister's chit-chat with the team.

What caught my attention was Mr. Rishabh Pant, an Indian wicketkeeper-batsman, who returned to the field with elan after a 14-month absence due to a life-threatening road accident in 2022, before the IPL.

No doubt, physios and coaches helped Pant a lot to overcome this adversity; the leading force in his recovery was Pant's commitment toward IPL, despite sustaining injuries, he remained resilient by motivating his mind with the field's charm to see himself on the field playing finally and his team lifting the Victory Cup. "

Any idea about the success mantra behind this jaw-dropping, outlandish skill of Pant to turn the tables in his favour?

This is a scientifically proven Concept of Brain phenomenon, i.e., 'neuroplasticity', which is derived from two words- neuro-nervous system + plasticity-change.

**NEUROPLASTICITY is the brain's ability to grow, adapt, and change.**

The brain is a highly active, malleable learning machine that weaves connections between existing neurons and prunes old, obsolete connections.

When we create a new connection, we experience consistent and positive energy changes that rewire and reshape the brain, leading to an 'ah-ha' moment.

Even small actions, such as finger movements, walking, breathing, and sleeping, depend on a healthy connection between the mind and body.

Rewiring the brain is the process that underlies biological self-determination, also known as self-directed neuroplasticity, which enables the formation of habits and a new identity.

Have you ever heard the saying, 'It takes 21 days to break or form a habit'?

In his book Atomic Habits, James Clear rightly mentions that if you get 1% worse each day for one year, you'll decline nearly to Zero.

Conversely, if you improve by 1% each day for one year, you'll emerge as a new person by the time you're done.

Because with small actions, the more evidence your neurons collect, the more intensely you will believe it. Our health requires changing our habits. The more you trigger neural pathways in the brain, the stronger they get.

**Rewiring the brain with Daily Self-Care-**

- Mind exercises - Improve your focus, concentration, and memory with daily mini 5-minute mental exercises or games, such as Sudoku, chess, or brushing your teeth with your non-dominant hand.

- Art & Music- Release stress through drawing, painting, or singing.
- Meditation- Reinforce neural pathways related to positive emotions.
- Yoga- Remind the brain to enjoy more mindful moments, connect with the body, and activate the vagus nerve.
- Learning new skills- Enhances brain plasticity, and you can remember because of the brain's ability to adapt to change.

Suppose you incorporate any one of the activities mentioned above into your self-care routine for just 5 minutes daily. In that case, the mind-body connection will gradually accumulate over the year, even if progress feels slow at first.

**Benefits of Rewiring-**

"Being a Health and wellness coach, one of our neighbours (Mohan) approached me (being a health and wellness coach) to help his wife come out of depression.Mohan is a Pilot in an established air company and earns a lofty package. He supports his aged parents, his wife (Pinki), and one teenage daughter.

Some years before, everything was alright at his home. As their daughter is growing, his Wife's naggling, irritations, anger, and continuous blabbering are increasing day by day. Her memory is weakening, and she has lost her appetite. She has chosen to seclude herself by locking herself in a room.

The doctor diagnosed her with the first stage of depression. Even medication was not improving her condition.The husband is mostly on flights, the teenage girl is busy with her friends, and her time is spent on household chores. She is left with no one to talk to or discuss her things/concerns, or to go out when she wants.

Slowly, she suppressed her loneliness. She watched daily soaps and thoroughly enjoyed their fancy life, where she was the only speaker.

So, I went to meet Pinki. She welcomed me with a big smile. Over tea, she started with her pet story and went on to complain about everyone and everything in her house.

**From our conversation, I learned that she has lost her identity in caring for her home, household chores, her parents, and her child.**

She surprised me with her hearty laugh while telling me about her favourite subjects, her interests, including drawing, book reading, and writing poems, as well as her favourite sport and her circle of friends.After much deliberation with Mohan, I asked Pinki to help me complete an Art project on Saturday.

The first week, she resisted, but seeing scattered colours every time near her mirror, she picked them and mesmerised me with her drawing finesse and colour teamwork.With God's grace, after six months' effort, Pinki is now returning to her real identity, lives in high esteem (from within) and her doctor has also reduced her dosage of medicines."

**Any guess? What helped Pinki to come out of the loop of self-limiting thoughts?**

Pinki rewired her brain to navigate herself from dependency to independence with-

- Medication
- Basic asanas to calm her mind first (to align with the body)
- Meditation & Affirmations,

- Created self-made boundaries (at what time to do household chores, at what time to do something of her own choice)
- Did journaling poetically (as she liked poem writing, you can choose your creative way)
- Looking at sunshine and moonlight occasionally.
- To understand the growing child's needs as per the present scenario and to befriend her.

So, this real-life incident indicates that REWIRING of the Brain helps to bring a shift in

- Increased capacity for healing
- Enhanced cognitive ability
- Clarity and inner calm
- Planning and achieving goals
- Adaptability and flexibility

**"Only by being obsessed with little things do great things emerge."** (Andy Dunn)

The mind and body are one functioning unit, with tangible links between our thoughts, emotions, and bodily alignment and balanced functions. The mind and emotions influence the body, as the body, in turn, influences the mind and emotions (Selhub, 2007).

Emotions manifest in the body as physical sensations, and physical sensations can produce corresponding emotions.

**Symptoms of a Mind-Body Connection Imbalance**

As I explained in the above case study, the mind-body connection imbalance led my neighbour into the self-made asylum of depression, which often ends in rehabilitation centres. Such imbalances impact people differently.

## i) Physical symptoms

- Gastrointestinal issues
- Chronic headaches
- Sleep issues, low energy
- Weight fluctuation
- High blood pressure
- Muscle tension
- Loss of appetite

## ii) Emotional and Mental Symptoms

- Depression, or mood swings
- Difficulty managing stress
- Adapting to life changes
- Inability to focus
- Excessive anxiety,
- Indecisive
- Maintaining healthy relationships.

The brain is so clever that when it regularly experiences stress, anger, jealousy, or similar emotions, it retains them and gradually transfers this burden to the heart or any other vulnerable part of the body.

It also ensures that a person responds in the same old pattern, whether through anxiety, yelling, people-pleasing, aggression, guilt, shame, or depression, whenever a particular situation arises, such as a fight, added work, stress, anger, jealousy, or stepping out of their comfort zone.

Additionally, it creates a fear of change, preventing the person from breaking the old pattern and adopting a new belief.If these emotions are not accepted and addressed, and self-care (to seek help from professionals) is not acted upon accordingly, you will keep floating in the loop of imbalanced mind and body functions.

"In August 2023, during my certification course in yoga, our trainers asked us to drink only normal water (instead of chilled/cold water from the fridge) for 21 days. I am a hardcore cold-water addict. So, for me, this was taming a bull.Regardless, I threw my hat in the air with pride and tamed it. No wonder I stumbled through this task with the bull so many times. I continued this practice even after the course, as it greatly benefited my digestive system.It was summer in 2024, and with the daily high temperature, I started gulping chilled water. Courtesy of my clever brain, I didn't notice falling again into the old pattern loop until my digestion issues said hello, and I was in front of a doctor."

Confused? Why did I start the old habit again, even after practising the new habit for one year?

**"Until you make the unconscious conscious, it will direct your life and you will call it fate."**- Carl Jung

This alert made me grab James Clear's "Atomic Habits", mentioning four laws of behaviour change.

James Clear's 4 Laws of Behaviour Change (to build better habits)

- **Cue**- Make it more obvious
- It is more like a signal to the brain to initiate a habit.
- **Craving**- Make it more attractive
- Like, motivation to do something you like.
- **Response**- Make it easy
- When you can do the thing you've been wanting to do.
- **Reward**- Make it satisfying
- Like a prize for completing the first three steps.

And I wanted this to remind me of the outcome I achieved with the application of the above rule's test.

Since most of my time is spent staring at the computer in the office's AC room, I hardly get out of my chair and hydrate myself. I placed an attractive blue colour glass bottle at an average temperature near my PC. **(Cue- made it more obvious)**

Now, it's so convenient that whenever I see the bottle, I feel the urge to grab it **(Craving—feeling the desire to drink water).**

Moreover, now my mind has realised that only normal water is near, so my body quickly accepts it.Bottle within my reach, I frequently drink the water **(Response - made it easy )**

The more I drink water, the more I have to visit the washroom.What surprised me was that in this way, not only do I keep myself hydrated, but I also keep my body moving and give my eyes a rest in between **(Reward—made it satisfying).**

My biggest lesson learnt from this?

**No behavioural shift happens in isolation. Instead, one leads to another.**

The outstanding result was the cue for my subsequent behaviour of being physically active, which began with simple strolling and culminated in a certified course in Yoga, followed by Kathak, and so on.

With each positive habit stacking, my mind is leading me to new possibilities of self-care, presenting a more polished version of myself with each higher step of self-discovery.Dust off self-defeating beliefs, look up for your microevolutions to be finally the new YOU, and start to

- Notice your thoughts, followed by the emotions they evoke, and then observe how you naturally behave in response.
- Think about who you want to be
- Prove it to yourself with small wins

**b) Self-Care- An antidote to Self-Sabotage**

Brianna Wiest, author of'The Mountain Is You' states that-**"Self-sabotage is just a maladaptive Coping mechanism. When we refuse to consciously meet our innermost needs, often because we do not believe we can handle them."**

Self-sabotage is a form of behavioral and thought deregulation, where you hinder your happiness and sense of accomplishment through blocks like ignorance, procrastination, unhealthy habits, work stress, financial struggles, time mismanagement, fear of change, and denial—particularly in relationships—as a way to protect yourself from perceived danger or harm.

Self-sabotage is a detrimental habit for self-.

- To believe they do not deserve happiness and success, and that they are not worthy of what they consciously try to achieve.
- To sacrifice one's happiness and well-being for others, with one's own wish, and feel proud of it.

And this habit pushes the self-saboteur in battling the storm of physical, mental, and emotional instability inside and living unfavourable situations, depression, burnouts, fears, anxiety outside.

**"A common type of self-saboteur is one who finds the price of hope too high to pay for." —The School of Life**

(Source: Google)

Moving out of a discomforting comfort situation leaves many in unknown fears irrespective of their education, status, religion, class, gender, age, country, etc.

Your self-sabotage occurs when you desire a change in yourself, your lifestyle, or your career, but are too afraid to act.And words like 'not me/ how me/ not for me' become the blocks of your life created not by others but by you, only to obstruct your way to live the optimum level of your highest good.

"In 2007, I was working as a clerk when the Departmental Promotion Committee approved my name for a promotion to Senior Assistant. As the news spread through the office, my colleagues congratulated me, but I was overwhelmed with fear. Ultimately, I decided to decline the promotion.

When my father found out, he asked me why I was choosing to forgo the opportunity to rise. I shared my fears and doubts, feeling incompetent, imperfect, and burdened by my family circumstances, including caring for my young child and elderly mother-in-law. I also mentioned my lack of knowledge and low confidence in speaking in front of officers.He asked me very simple questions:-

> After getting married, who taught me to cook food for not only my family but also guests?

My reply - By applying my mind and drawing on my experience.

>After marriage, how did I end up washing both my and my husband's clothes (when before marriage, I couldn't even bring myself to wash a small handkerchief), and that too without a washing machine?

My reply - By applying my mind and drawing on my experience.

>After becoming a mother, who taught me how to care for a baby, feed him, and look after his needs?

My reply: By applying my own mind and drawing on experience.

>How did I earn my Master's degree in Commerce in one go from one of India's elite universities, Punjab University, Chandigarh?

My reply- With my intelligence and efforts.

>Did my education in one of the most highly literate cities, Chandigarh (the education hub), not help me understand facts better than others?

My reply- Absolutely.

Then he very gently explained, "See, after marriage, you automatically realised your responsibilities and performed them so well on your own with your knowledge, with self-learnt experiences. And we are so proud of our daughter."

He also made me realise that when I would be promoted to a higher position, my mind would automatically begin to function more intelligently. With his renewed confidence in me, I decided to seize the opportunity to rise higher in 2008. "

Since then, with each subsequent promotion, I have always shared the divine magic of my achievements first with my father. Even after achieving education and a job through my intelligence and honest efforts, I still became doubtful of my capacity to handle higher responsibilities.

However, by stepping out of my comfort zone and fuelling myself with self-confidence, I allowed myself to leap. This consistent growth eventually led me to a senior position, where I could enjoy the benefits of my work and feel completely at ease.

**The Mountain Is You** by Brianna Wiest focuses on this type of block between you and the life you want to live, and offers tangible solutions to help you transcend it.

The metaphor of the mountain is used to represent both external challenges and internal obstacles that we face throughout our lives. These mountains are barriers that we erect for ourselves, arising from traumas, environments, relationships, and so on.

This book delves into some common real-life mountains like -

- Perfectionism
- Setting upper limits (to feel happy)
- Emotional triggers
- Procrastination etc.

"At home, I would yell at my three hyperactive Boys, two of my sons and one, my mother-in-law's son, who happens to be my husband, for cleaning the messy kitchen, room, washrooms, and clothes stacking.At the office, I wanted each item on my table to be in its fixed place and a fixed direction. A 'boss is always right' attitude, combined with perfectionism, would make my staff anxious, confused, and annoyed.I wanted to spend time with my family and be the cool boss in the office, but failing to keep everything in order was infuriating, leading to more burnouts and a feeling of failure. Family and staff labelled me a nag. "

So, I applied the key solutions from the book mentioned above to address my perfectionism, which has become similar to OCD.

**i) I tuned in to connecting with myself first to listen to my inner thoughts.**

>Accepted the whirl of emotions in mind and body.

- How am I mainly feeling?

- Which part of my body is getting stretched or tensed? Mind or body?

> Jotted down all my emotions in the current scenario.

- What was I feeling?
- Am I angry or feeling like crying?
- I am angry because -

#Feeling helpless to keep everything organised as I want?

#Feeling my authority is at stake?

#Feeling the situation getting out of my control?

#Is this my ego or self-respect?

**ii) I reflected on my experiences of successes and failures.**

- Anxiety and burnout immediately chained me in a vicious Loop of high, unattainable expectations and failures to meet them that were leaving me in a pool of unrealistic fears.
- The reason was that I wanted everything to be as I liked; I ignored the whistle, as my mind and body were overwhelmed by the impending danger.
- Completely lost the connection with the power of my inbuilt virtues and couldn't listen to my inner voice and wisdom.
- I was chasing an elusive self-imposed standard that I, as well as others, have to meet at any cost.

**iii) Through self-examination, I discovered that my cleanliness habit had evolved into excessive cleanliness, and perfectionism was stemming from OCD in my genes.**

- With inner motivations, I dived deeper and found that OCD was a direct result of my childhood conditioning.
- I wanted everything to be in my way only, as I doubt other people's capabilities and felt ashamed to accept someone else's idea.
- Under the carpet, I was doing everything possible to make others feel proud of me. Behind this pattern was the fear of being disliked by others.
- In this way, I was continuously caring for others' validation, and my sense of well-being was not on my agenda.

**IV) I worked on my conditioning.**

- The guidance of an experienced professional initially helped me reconnect with myself.
- Reach the root of my trauma since my inception in the womb and rewired the neurons to cleanse it, to break the old patterns.
- Learnt to let go of all pebbles connected with this conditioning.
- I practised related meditations to heal my inner child and set myself free from unwanted baggage.
- I established a forgiveness routine and replaced it with unconditional love.

**v ) Neurological rewiring.**

- Inner cleansing paved the way for me to shift my attention towards the lessons from my mistakes.
- Made conscious choices to focus on a new, realistic goal aligned with my authentic self.

- Intentionally trained my brain to focus more on progress than perfection
- Small steps, even if they seem insignificant, are still steps forward.
- Developed a new habit of not judging anyone, including myself.

**vi) Celebrated small victories.**

- I discovered a newfound sense of self-worth and a deeper understanding of my capabilities.
- Incremental positive changes resulted in the freedom to fly with your self-created wings of newly developed skills.
- Validating my achievement and celebrating each victory with a reward (mind only registers the reward) boosted my confidence.
- In my case, now I enjoy more quality time with my family,

My personal experience would help you to get a clear idea that:-

- Self-abandonment is the root of self-sabotage, as it starts when you stop listening to your inner voice. It involves suppressing your needs, happiness, and feelings while ignoring emotional and physical bruises or declining health under various pretexts.
- Develop self-awareness to quietly observe and accept disturbing thoughts, emotions, behaviours, patterns, and fears as they arise, without judgment.
- By nipping turbulent behaviours and patterns in the bud with self-compassion and resilience, we can smoothly

move from where we are now to where we want to be.

Keep the unwavering faith deep within you that, with perseverance and consistent actions, and conscious, positive thoughts focused on self-care, you will transform self-sabotage into Self-Mastery.

As Marcus Aurelius says, **"The impediment to action advances action. What stands in the way becomes the way."**

We can't improve what we don't

assess

(author-Micael Hyatt)

# Chapter 4: Self-Assessment of Self-Care

What comes to your mind when you see a tree in the following two images?

Image 1

(Source:Sora)

Image 2

(Source: sora)

What kind of tree would you resonate with?

*Image-1*- The one who is strong and dense enough to give shade (happiness) to so many people conveniently.

OR

*Image-2*- The one who is sparse and good for nothing for even a single person.

**"A tree that refuses water and sunlight for herself can't bear fruit for others"** -Emily Maroutian.

- Suppose you resonate with Image 1- **Congratulations!** However, continue to work on your self-care consistently to maintain your high self-esteem.
- If you identify your situation in image 2, **start working on your self-care before it's too late! And even yourself is not happy with yourself.**

**"You can't build joy on a feeling of self-loathing."** (unknown)

- As discussed in previous chapters, self-care is nothing but taking a pause,
- To assess the peace and happiness of your mind and body.
- It will help you maintain your well-being across various health dimensions, even amidst your personal and professional commitments in multiple roles.

*>> Have you ever assessed your health at following areas-*
*psychological (mind)
*Physical (body)
*Emotional
*Spiritual

*Workplace
*Social
*Environmental
>>If you have not, then -

- To identify the areas of your identity that need improvement and the strengths to be enhanced, a one-minute assessment of your behaviour and actions is required.
- Take a cup of Coffee, sit in a comfortable place, and score your behaviour/action/feeling in the following sheets on a scale of 1 -5

5=Always
4 = often
3 = Sometimes
2 = Rarely
1 = Never

- Rules of Game-

i) No self's or others' judging/blaming
ii) honest rating
Tables
**i) Psychological (mind) Self-Care -**

| ACTIVITY | Always | Often | Sometimes | Rarely | Never |
|---|---|---|---|---|---|
| Fully present (on any activity or conversation), mentally alert and sharp in the moment | | | | | |
| | | | | | |
| When faced with stress/problem-<br>• I panic<br>• I reaffirm I can handle this<br>• Learn lessons from setbacks | | | | | |
| Spend *time with me doing nothing* (e.g. *staring in any direction without any motive/intention)* | | | | | |
| Journaling (in any form, story, lines, poetry, colouring, sketch drawing) | | | | | |
| Book reading | | | | | |
| Listen to my inner voice (thoughts, judgements, beliefs, attitudes, etc.) | | | | | |
| My success or behaviour depends on others' validation | | | | | |
| Keep a list of methods always handy to shift the energy/thought process of my mind in stress and counsel myself if needed | | | | | |
| Keep learning something new or even reconnecting to an old interest | | | | | |
| Meditate / breathing | | | | | |
| Connect with nature (sunshine, clouds, birds, looking at the moon, stars, galaxy) | | | | | |
| Take out time to play games or mind exercises to keep my mind and memory sharp. | | | | | |
| Make sure not to sleep with complaints against someone in mind, rather forgive and let go | | | | | |
| Other | | | | | |

## ii) Physical (body) Self-Care-

| ACTIVITY | Always | Often | Sometimes | Rarely | Never |
|---|---|---|---|---|---|
| Level of energy throughout a typical day (energy booster, energy drain, etc)<br>• Low<br>• high |  |  |  |  |  |
| I am high in -<br>• Confidence<br>• Motivation<br>• Work performance<br>• self-efficacy |  |  |  |  |  |
| Weight management |  |  |  |  |  |
| I enjoy my three meals (breakfast, lunch and dinner)<br>• Without TV/phone<br>• With TV /phone |  |  |  |  |  |
| Keep checking my nutrition (consumption of) -<br>• healthy snacks,<br>• Fruit<br>• Water<br>• soft/alcoholic drinks<br>• Refined carbs |  |  |  |  |  |
| Take leave when needed |  |  |  |  |  |
| • Exercise regularly (yoga, walking in nature, etc.)<br>• On cheat days, I move my body a bit but make sure to move |  |  |  |  |  |
| Sound sleep<br>• When I woke up, I felt refreshed and rejuvenated |  |  |  |  |  |
| Detoxify from electronic devices |  |  |  |  |  |
| Enjoy weekends/vacations with me and my family |  |  |  |  |  |
| Medical checkups/medications |  |  |  |  |  |
| Hot oil massage |  |  |  |  |  |
| Walking barefoot on grass |  |  |  |  |  |
| Feeling the breeze on the skin |  |  |  |  |  |

## iii) Emotional Self-Care

| ACTIVITY | Always | Often | Sometimes | Rarely | Never |
|---|---|---|---|---|---|
| I am good at<br>• Coping skills to handle stress or sudden challenges in life<br>• Resilience<br>• Handling Stress | | | | | |
| Listen, accept, acknowledge the exact word for the Feelings, fears, doubts, etc | | | | | |
| Daily affirm with positive self-beliefs/self-talk to charge my energy high for the whole day | | | | | |
| Allow me to cry, find the reasons and work accordingly.<br>• In a hurtful moment, I give a self-soothing touch to help me feel comforted and safe. | | | | | |
| Do things that make me laugh from the heart | | | | | |
| Express my anger softly but sternly | | | | | |
| Keep exploring ways to express my creativity (writing, painting, sewing, drawing, playing an instrument, dancing etc.) | | | | | |
| On experiencing a bad situation in the day, feel the exact emotion and flip it into a positive one and show gratitude before sleeping | | | | | |
| Keep healing the inner wounds | | | | | |
| Forgive myself easily | | | | | |
| Love myself unconditionally (i.e. I am comfortable with my flaws) | | | | | |
| Know how and when to say a clear NO | | | | | |
| My boundaries are non-negotiable | | | | | |
| know my needs | | | | | |
| My sole motive is to keep my inner peace intact, *no matter what* | | | | | |
| Aware of what people/ content create stress in me<br>• My modus operandi is ready to deal with them | | | | | |
| Know how to protect my happiness | | | | | |
| Money is-<br>• Demon<br>• Loving energy | | | | | |

| | | |
|---|---|---|
| My internal support is strong enough to respond to the world in healthier ways (e.g brisk walking, 5-minute conscious breathing, shifting mind focus on something else like a particular colour etc.) | | |
| other | | |

## iv) Spiritual Self-Care

| ACTIVITY | Always | Often | Sometimes | Rarely | Never |
|---|---|---|---|---|---|
| Satisfaction in terms of-<br>• Life<br>• Work<br>• Personal relationship<br>• Family<br>• blessings | | | | | |
| Keep marking what is truly meaningful to me in life | | | | | |
| Find ways to connect to my higher self, the ultimate supreme power, with prayer, meditation, singing, dancing, writing letters, | | | | | |
| Read and/or listen to things that maintain my faith in divine powers, unwavering | | | | | |
| Respect, help and be kind to each child of God | | | | | |
| Bless the other person (not favourable for me) for the goodness of God that is within him | | | | | |
| Find a spiritual connection or community online or offline | | | | | |
| On so so-so-not-so-good day, rewind the bad situation and forgive, bless and let go and surrender | | | | | |
| Other: | | | | | |

## v) Workplace Self-Care

| ACTIVITY | Always | Often | Sometimes | Rarely | Never |
|---|---|---|---|---|---|
| Take breaks at regular intervals | | | | | |
| Sometimes enjoy chatting (not gossip/backbite) with positive-minded colleagues or co-workers | | | | | |
| Identify projects or tasks that are exciting and rewarding | | | | | |
| Balance my workload | | | | | |
| Organise my workspace to be comfortable and pleasing | | | | | |
| Respond more than react | | | | | |
| Negotiate for my needs (e.g. benefits, pay raise, etc.) | | | | | |
| Maintain a support system with seniors and/or co-workers | | | | | |
| Keep my family and profession separate | | | | | |
| Keep my boundaries non-negotiable with colleagues/clients/subordinates | | | | | |

## vi) Social Self-Care

| ACTIVITY | Always | Often | Sometimes | Rarely | Never |
|---|---|---|---|---|---|
| Spend time with the tribe of my vibe | | | | | |
| Spend quality time with children/family | | | | | |
| Spend time with animals (pets) | | | | | |
| Have a strong support system to help me at any time without judging me | | | | | |
| A healthy relationship with family | | | | | |
| A healthy relationship with friends | | | | | |
| People in my society, area, know me and have a good rapport with me | | | | | |
| Enjoy meeting new people | | | | | |
| Remove toxic friends/people from my life not serve my highest good | | | | | |
| Others | | | | | |

## vii) Environmental Self-Care

| ACTIVITY | Always | Often | Sometimes | Rarely | Never |
|---|---|---|---|---|---|
| Do activities that are more environmentally friendly | | | | | |
| Do activities that are more earth-friendly | | | | | |
| Avoid hoarding unnecessary shopping for clothes | | | | | |
| Enjoy the activities that are directly related to environmental protection (planting trees, promoting paperless work, etc) | | | | | |
| Community clean-ups | | | | | |
| Switch off electric appliances (in the house/office) when not required | | | | | |
| Switch off Wi-Fi/networks (of the house) before slipping into bed | | | | | |
| others | | | | | |

Let's check your score-

- 75-95 (impossible to score 100 in real life) voila! Great gun!! Keep going.
- 65-74 - on the way to master self-care!! Keep going.
- 55-64- novice self-care! Keep moving.
- Below 55, aware of self-care terms but lack the know-how! Seek support from peers, a strong support system, and professionals to improve self-care

Let us analyse your self-care score in different contexts on the above parameters at a glance (details to be discussed in an upcoming chapter).

**I) Emotional Self-Care:**

If you're scoring low in this area, it highlights a key aspect of your emotional health that needs improvement.

Emotional health refers to a person's ability to think, feel, and cope effectively in both positive and negative situations, as well as with different people.

*Start with-*

- Analyse your relationship with yourself and in your relationships in a more realistic manner.
- Stare at your emotions to accept them; it will also help to find the exact solution.
- Contact a therapist if needed
- Go for a long drive of your interest

### ii) Psychological Self-Care:

If your rating is low in this area, it indicates a need to work on your psychological health.Psychological health focuses on emotional, cognitive, behavioural, and social well-being. When our psychological state is imbalanced, we may struggle with indecisiveness, managing emotions, controlling behaviours, interacting with others, and handling stress or other challenges.

*Start with -*

- Add the activities that enable you to think critically, find quick solutions, and learn in changing times.
- Reading books is a mental exercise to sharpen memory and learning abilities.

### iii) Physical self-care:

If you're scoring low, it's time to take action and start engaging in physical activities to improve your physical health. Bodily health refers to the condition of your body, its ability to heal itself, and its resistance to illness.

**It can be by being-**

- Physically active
- Practice healthy habits
- Ability to heal, get good sleep
- Walk while you talk

- Avoid toxic/ unnecessary invitations

**iv) Spiritual self-care (Health):**

If you're scoring low in this area, your spiritual health is out of balance. Spiritual health involves having a strong mindset, leading a meaningful life, cultivating altruism and ethics, and developing a sense of purpose that fosters peace and resilience.

It's about believing in your ability to thrive and navigate life with practices *such as:*

- Meditation
- Prayer
- Connecting the mind and body to set and work toward life goals
- For atheists, reconnecting with core values that define you as a good person and human
- Practising gratitude by acknowledging 3-5 things each morning or bedtime that make you feel alive

**V) Social self-care**

Low social health impacts your mental health, physical health and mortality risk.

Social health refers to the ability to interact and form meaningful relationships with others in a comfortable manner.

*Develop it by -*

- Creating a support system of meaningful, loving, helping, and kind 3 AM friends/people
- Talk to your friends who uplift you without showing/ judging you
- Be in contact with a healthy friendship

- Join some clubs, online / offline, like-minded communities
- Meet new people with wisdom
- Reach out to people you have not seen for quite long
- Serve people with kindness and compassion

**VI) Environmental Self-Care:**

A low score in environmental self-care indicates a disconnection from nature. We cannot live happily on Earth without taking care of our environment, as every drop is essential for filling the ocean.

A clean environment provides the benefits of fresh air, clean water, and healthy soil. If the climate is unhealthy, with toxic chemicals and pollution contaminating our resources, our health suffers as well.

Environmental health focuses on the relationship between human health and the environment, including both natural and human-made environments, and their impact on overall well-being.

*Be more earth and environmentally friendly with-*

- For markets or nearby places, walk
- Opt for outdoor sports
- In apt weather, go for planting trees wherever possible
- Switch off unnecessary lights
- Stop wasting water

These are some everyday activities for better self-care, but remember that one size does not fit all. Activities are tailored to the uniqueness of each individual and their environment, allowing their souls to shine.

**"Every act of self-care is a powerful declaration:**

I am on my side, I am on my side, Each day, I am more and more on my side."
— Susan Weiss Berry

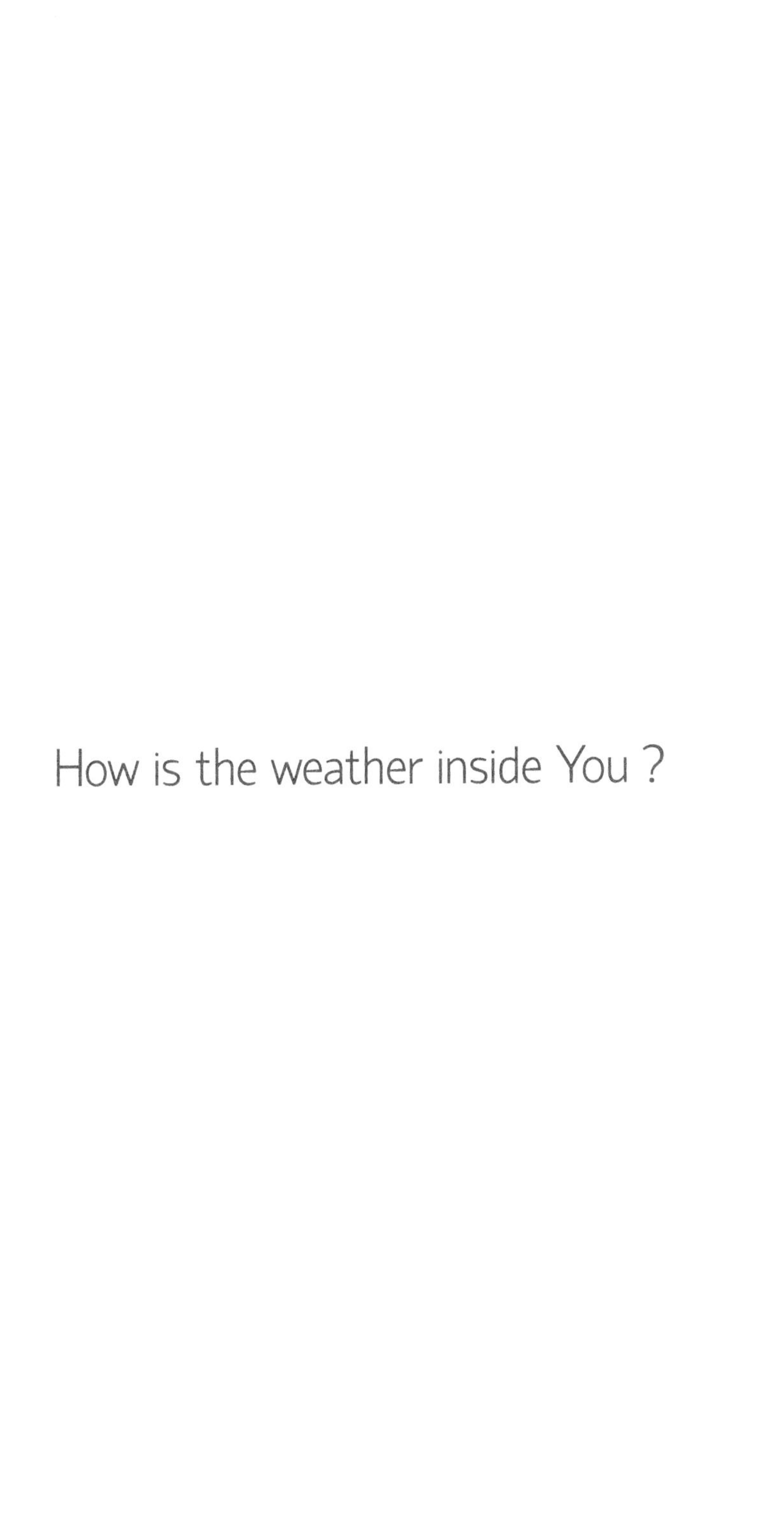
How is the weather inside You ?

# Chapter 5: Emotional Assessment Wheel

**"Listen to your emotions first to make sense of self-care."**
- Unknown

The self-care assessment has made it clear that emotions play a significant role in our lives, acting as a mode of communication between us and the environment or world around us. This communication creates different energy levels, and your mind and body respond to these energies through various sensations at different moments and across other areas of life.

Your behaviour is shaped by the beliefs you have internalised based on these emotions and feelings from childhood up to the present.

The environment surrounding you during childhood, when your mind is still in its formative stage, either empowers you to recognise and express your feelings openly or leaves you struggling to identify and articulate what you are feeling. This, in turn, shapes your beliefs, which solidify into your identity.

Understanding and analyzing this process reveals that your beliefs form the foundation of who you are today. Labelling your emotions correctly acts as a ventilator, allowing the light of the actual cause to enter and enabling the rewiring process to occur, accompanied by the appropriate healing actions.

"I recall when I was preparing for my commerce exams in 1985. Overconfident and unprepared, I had not studied well, and as a result, I struggled even to score minimal marks. I was granted a mercy chance to appear for the final exam, but my father set a strict ultimatum- either pass the exam or be ready for marriage. There were only two months left before the exam.

This jolt terrified me, and I confined myself in my room **(situation A)** with fear. I would move out, when necessary, only to pass each day in fear. I also stopped having a meal on one pretext or another.

As earlier, I used to sit alone for hours **(situation B)**. So, no one became suspicious of my behaviour.

After one month, I suddenly fainted. When I was taken to the hospital, the doctor informed my parents that my pulse rate was very slow, my body was dehydrated and weak due to insufficient food, and that my body was in a state of fear. However, my family was completely clueless about the situation.

Once I regained consciousness, I explained to the doctor and my family about the fear I had been living with, which left my parents in utter shock and regret. The doctor then took the time to counsel both me and my parents.

At home, my father sat beside me and said that he knew I was a hard worker and that through hard work alone, I would carve out a niche for myself. With teary eyes, he told me that he knew I deserved the best future, which could only be achieved through a good education.

He then made me promise that, in the future, I would always share my emotions, fears, and thoughts first with either my mother or father, without hesitation, and that we would never judge me for anything.

This conversation reignited my confidence, and as a result, I passed the exam with a very good score.

If you compare the above marked Situation-A and Situation-B, both are similar, as in both situations, I sat alone.But the emotions in both situations are different.

After working on my emotional self-care, I discovered that,

- **Situation A** is 'Loneliness', where each day is filled with fear and shame, feeling suffocated by overthinking imaginary future fears, asking, 'What if this happens?' or 'What if that happens?' This leads to low self-esteem.
- **Situation B** is 'Solitude', where I enjoy the peace of nature, the silence of my room, and my own company, all while experiencing a sense of high self-esteem.

Had my parents and I been aware of the correct emotions, the situation would have been entirely different at that time."

Though emotion is commonly described in terms of:

- Joy
- Love
- Fear
- Anger
- Sad
- Surprise

These emotions are deeply tied to feelings from childhood. To receive the best treatment, an accurate diagnosis is essential.For example, frustration is linked to anger, and the core emotion of rejection is sadness. Without understanding the root of these emotions, finding a way out is like navigating a maze. To simplify this, refer to the emotional assessment wheel below, which has been helpful to me.

# Wheel Of Emotions

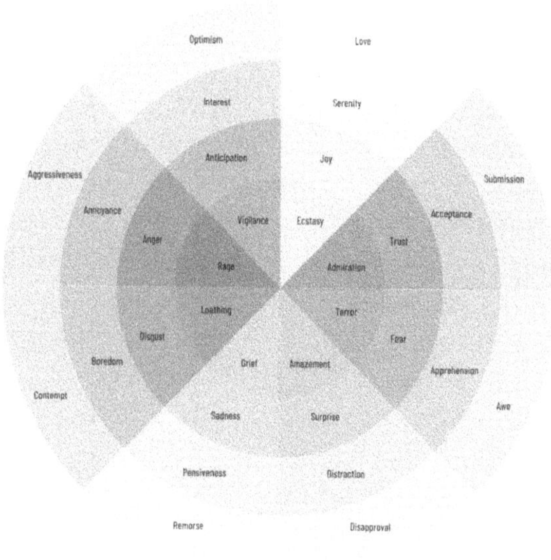


(source:Canva)

To figure out the exact cause to remove, just start your search by proceeding with the following steps:

**i) Labelling-**

- In other words, the process of identifying exactly what we are feeling.

- Correct emotion will be our driving force to act upon

## ii) Acting

- Now find the intensity of emotions (1-10) to make us understand how deeply we are feeling that emotion.
- Accordingly, the next course of action is to be decided
- It requires either inner changes or outer changes; i.e., the need is required within us, so an action plan or professional help is needed.
- For some, even spiritual practices, such as chanting and connecting with the higher self, may be beneficial.

## iii) Healing process of faith

We are all different, so is the other mindset programming. Therefore, we all have different capacities to handle problems.

If the prints of your disturbing emotions are not deeply embedded, the healing will occur sooner.If there are underlying issues, we must maintain faith that with consistent practice, we will overcome them.Healing time depends on one's upbringing, genetics, struggles, relationships, and surroundings.

It is quite possible that taking action settles your inner ambivalence to some extent, but at least it will bring more equanimity.Keep working with faith, small achievements are stacking the foundation of inner happiness forever.

As Brianna Wiest eloquently expresses in her exceptional book The Mountain Is You: **"Personal growth sprouts from the soil of understanding and accepting your own emotions."**

Self-Esteem comes from being able to do Self-Care with Self-Love on your terms.

# Chapter 6: Self-Care, Self-Love & Self-Esteem

"Acknowledge, accept, and honour that you deserve your own deepest compassion and love."

— Nanette Mathews

**Connection between self-care, self-love, and self-esteem**

- Self-care is the practice of taking actions that help maintain personal health and balance, replenish energy and motivation, and foster growth, ultimately leading to balanced self-esteem and increased self-love.
- Self-love is a profound mental state of unconditional acceptance and appreciation for your flaws and imperfections. It nurtures self-esteem and confidence by cultivating a positive self-image.
- Self-esteem is often rooted in how we evaluate our worth and value based on our achievements, rather than seeking approval from others.

The most crucial element of self-care is self-love. Therefore, respect your well-being every day, in every moment, and at every place.

In your youth and adulthood, you've likely built a sandcastle on the beach. Does it stay intact when a strong storm hits?

Now, imagine if that sandcastle represented you. What would your strategy be?

- Would you allow the waves of unhappiness to wash it away?

*OR*

- Would you protect your happiness by caring for your dignity, respect, and inner peace?

I believe you would choose the second option.
***The Basic rules*** *to build a strong foundation of self-care:*
I) Acceptance:
**"Because one believes in oneself, one doesn't try to convince others. Because one is content with oneself, one doesn't need others' approval. Because one accepts oneself, the whole world accepts him or her."**— Lao Tzu.

Acceptance may sound like a pill to pop down, but it is that dreaded surgery of our thoughts about ourselves, which, if not done, may turn into a fatal disease called Self-Sabotage.

"If one thing Corona left in me, it was my deteriorating hair.My long, voluminous hair pleat was losing its sheen and becoming so brittle that it seemed to beautify the floor more than my scalp. On my dermatologist's advice, I renounced hair colour (with a heavy heart) until my hair became healthy again.

I hid my face from the mirror, sulking over my white hairs, when the news of the marriage of the son of a close relative pierced my ears. I felt like a trapped mouse, with the options of either attending the wedding with grey hair or flaunting blonde and deep brown locks at the cost of irreparably damaging my hair.

When my dermatologist bombarded me with the side effects of colouring my hair again, I was left with no choice but to skip colouring and a series of questions:

- How would I face everyone at the wedding? They would tease me.
- How would I look wearing a beautiful dress with grey hair? I would be the odd one out.
- Maybe someone would call me 'Auntie'? How would I react?
- How would I explain to everyone why I'm not colouring my hair (as if it is mandatory for ladies in their fifties)?
- Would I look good with grey hair?

All these doubts, with the wedding day fast approaching, threw me into a loop of anxiety and indecision. Unable to bear the stress, I lay quietly, focusing solely on my breathing to calm my mind. It tranquillised me, and I regained my inner peace and confidence.

With that newfound sense of calm, I went to the mirror and looked at my wet hair after washing it. A realisation dawned upon me, whenever I wash my hair, the natural long waves give the appearance of permed hair. Many of my acquaintances were envious of that. This realisation marked the end of my sobbing story and the beginning of my shining story.

I found myself booking four weekend sessions of a simple hair spa (a kind of treatment) consisting of oiling with natural oils, massaging, hair steaming, and shampoo, all for just 500 bucks. After two weeks, I noticed a noticeable improvement in the look of my hair.

While enjoying my free time at the salon, I was flipping through the pages of a magazine on the best-dressed women. One of the contestants' styles sparked my creative cells. The contestant was young, yet she had chosen to colour her hair grey for her ramp walk, and here I was, trying to hide the grace I had cultivated over the years.

After this, I felt like Cinderella, who had found her missing shoe of confidence.At the wedding, I entered the dazzling venue with elan. I could feel that everyone was spellbound by my six-yard magic, with my flowy, open, long grey hair.

From worrying about covering my head, I became a head-turner, with everyone thinking I had deliberately coloured my hair grey as a fashion statement. I walked like a ramp queen through the entire wedding event, head held high."

Just think, how did I turn doubts into accolades? This magic was woven through Acceptance. When I accepted and loved my grey hair, it automatically gave me the confidence and ideas to flaunt my long grey hair with grace and become a fashion diva.

## II) Forgiveness

I.e., forgive yourself and move on.Forgive others and move on.If you love yourself, you learn to forgive others smoothly, and in this way, you will not carry others' baggage.By doing this, you will create a comfortable living space.

Forgiveness works in steps:

- Acceptance that you have done something bad or wrong, or against your ethics (intentionally or unintentionally). This will calm your mind first.
- Acknowledge your emotions (even the negative ones) to prevent your conscious mind from self-bashing and throwing you into a dark pit of guilt.
- Release the negative emotions with self-compassion, allowing yourself to make mistakes, just as others do. You are also a regular, flawed human being.
- Take responsibility for changing your wrong actions and be kind to yourself without judgment.
- Learn the lesson and refill your inner vessel with powerful affirmations to create intentional thoughts that break the old pattern.
- If possible, learn different forgiveness techniques online and practice those that are easiest for you (e.g., EFT, Hawaiian prayer of forgiveness, Ho'oponopono, breathing patterns).

Some affirmations you can use to build self-worth and make your belief stronger:

- I am human, and I make mistakes too.
- I forgive myself for what I did.
- This mistake is not my identity.
- I let go of feelings of guilt and shame.
- I forgive myself and others with ease.

Only forgiveness can unload the baggage of guilt, shame, and so on, creating the space for unconditional self-love within yourself and leading to greater happiness in your life.

The more you work on self-forgiveness for yourself first, the more you will be enabled to forgive others daily, both personally and professionally.

Forgiving others who have hurt you can be a challenging task, depending on the severity of the situation.

But remember the old saying, **'Practice makes the man perfect.'**

Let us take a walk down memory lane to our childhood:

- Sit on a chair with your feet flat on the floor.
- Close your eyes gently.
- Take 3-5 regular breaths.
- Mentally search and bring up an image of yourself as a child, between 5 to 10 years old, that you like the most.
- Now, visualise yourself running very fast on the playground, barefoot, feeling the sand and stones beneath your feet.
- While running, you spot a big puddle on the road and start jumping in it, laughing loudly with your friends.
- Suddenly, a strong push makes you fall into the puddle with a thud.
- You are hurt, crying, but your friends are looking at you, laughing and teasing you, yet no one lifts you.
- Now, think about what you would do in this situation:-

*Would you keep crying and lying on the ground, unable to get up because of the embarrassment of

being so weak, expecting your friends to lift you?

 OR

*Would you stay in the dirty water, accuse your friend of making you fall, and throw dirty water

at them?

OR

* Would you think, "So what if I fell?" Gather strength to stand tall, dust off your clothes, look at

your bruises, step out of the muddy water, and slowly walk away from that place.

Now, think about it: if this were your real-life situation and you found yourself in an unwanted circumstance, what would you do?

To learn forgiveness, or any practice, there's no magic wand to make it work for you. The only key is the ingredient of patience and perseverance, which helps build your forgiveness muscle and allows you to keep moving forward to live a fulfilled life filled with overflowing love.

Ever-increasing self-love will automatically enhance your self-esteem.

Self-esteem encompasses a sense of competence, belonging, security, self-confidence, and one's overall self-view.

The only thing you usually do in the face of harsh realities is abandon yourself, which becomes the starting point to sink even deeper into darkness.

However, if you hold onto self-love, it will lift you with better self-esteem, allowing you to make more informed choices for your self-care.

**"Once you loosen up and give yourself the wings of self-care, the sky is the limit."** (unknown)

What is stopping you to do Self-Care? guilt, unmotivated, No-worth, fear of change, Unaware?

# Chapter 7: Barriers of Self-Care

**"If you want to fly, you have to give up what weighs you down."**- Roy T. Bennett

How beautiful is the creation of The Ultimate Artist (the Universe) in the form of the butterfly, with its enchanting colours!

Close your eyes and think back to when you were a child- how excited you were to run after and dream of flying with the fancy butterflies hopping from flower to flower.

We enjoy watching these naturally designed winged creatures, but as Maya Angelou says: **"We delight in the beauty of the butterfly, but rarely admit the changes it has gone through to achieve that beauty."**

This is very true! We love the beauty, but often overlook the efforts it takes from inception to conclusion.

Your inner sanctuary blossoms with happiness, calmness, and more only through perseverance and persistence in taking good care of your emotions at all times.

"I was born on September 13th. As I stepped into my teens, I learned from my friends and neighbours that the number 13 was considered unlucky. It was so widely believed that even in flights, there were no seats with this number.

Although my parents never subscribed to this idea and always dismissed the topic, my young mind absorbed this thought. I began to think that my 'unlucky' factor was responsible for my struggles with intelligence, difficulty in communicating with people, not being good-looking, and feeling like no one wanted to talk to me.

Though my parents were born in the '50s, their thoughts were so ahead of their time that they would keep telling me that this belief was illogical. They believed that every outcome depended solely on our mindset. On the other hand, every minor disturbing situation seemed to confirm my belief in being 'unlucky.'

This continued until I discovered 'The Secret' by Rhonda Byrne. The book described that our experiences are merely the result of our own minds' thoughts. To test the truth of this, I started affirming: *"I am a magnet of success in everything I do."*

I recorded this affirmation in my voice and played it on repeat, at a whispering volume, throughout the day. After 40 days of continuous affirmation, I began to experience shifts in my confidence.This newfound confidence erased my self-limiting beliefs on various levels and uplifted my self-esteem. Gradually, my old belief of being "unlucky" transformed into the realisation that I was a 'blessed child of God'.

You are incredibly powerful by divine virtue, but due to social and environmental conditioning, you often create barriers that suppress your inner voice, which is meant to guide you in the best possible way.

By neglecting to take care of yourself promptly, you allow yourself to become a victim in various situations, leading to stress, low self-esteem, and a diminished sense of life satisfaction. This imbalance affects your spiritual, physical, and mental health.

Despite its significance, self-care is often overlooked, as individuals encounter numerous barriers that make it difficult to prioritise their personal needs.

The **most common barriers** include:

**1. Lack of time**

- In my Health and wellness coaching, every other client finds this barrier the culprit.
- In today's fast-paced life, they often find little time to fulfil their daily responsibilities, so where is the time for self-care?
- Their primary concern is that we work, have a family with ageing parents, our kids still need that care, our jobs have longer working hours, and we need to run a household.
- Time becomes the biggest reason for each age and gender strata.
- To all of them, my advice is to embrace flexibility.

*How to dismantle this barrier:*

- First, note down your time schedules from morning to evening.
- Then note down –Which area do you want to heal or take care of first? Start with a small and realistic change (something that is not imposed on you by someone else, nor intended to prove anything to anyone) so that it becomes sustainable.

- Identify the time gap when you can fit in an activity that aligns with your desired change.
- Consider what activities you can consistently start during that time. For example:
- Take a few deep breaths in the car before heading to work.
- Play your favourite song on your way home to unwind before transitioning into family mode.
- Recite a mantra as soon as you wake up.
- As my Yoga Training school founder, Mr. Ashok, says, "Solo is boring." Include your loved ones and have fun while working. So, if you have young children to care for, bring them along! For example, go for a walk with the kids, try some simple jumping or dancing to a song, or engage in creative activities together.
- Try to organise your kids' uniforms, your clothes, and prepare food in the evening. This will save you time in the morning and allow you to relax for a bit.

If your life requires extra family time, remember that your body needs more movement than others to recharge to its optimum level.

"When one of my clients, Ms. Shreshtha, came to me, family responsibilities and tuition classes consumed her entire day (both online and offline). She had gained weight, and her sugar levels had dropped to a dangerously low point. Her family was insisting that she stop her tuition, but she didn't want to lose her only source of income or her health, all while staying at home.

The question of 'how?' was disturbing her.After much deliberation, it became clear that she was waking up at 7 AM and immediately diving into work. We decided to make a small change; she would wake up just 15 minutes earlier and start with simple walk-walk steps for 5-10 minutes.

Over time, she gradually increased her wake-up time, and her self-motivation sparked a radical change in her self-esteem.Now, she is learning Yoga from me and enjoying everything, from family responsibilities to her classes, and has achieved optimum health."

## 2. Lack of self-compassionCompassion

Compassion occurs when you seize every opportunity to help someone in distress. Self-compassion, however, happens when you show yourself the same kindness by accepting your flaws, weaknesses, limitations, failures, or difficulties.

The irony is that we often take others unconditionally, but when it comes to ourselves, we become harsh and continue to bash ourselves.

When you practice more self-compassion, it builds resilience, allowing you to recover more quickly from any failure, embarrassment, or trauma.

**"If your compassion does not include yourself, it is incomplete."**- Jack Kornfield

*How to dismantle this barrier:*

- Grow your self-compassion muscle with:
- Self-kindness: Allow yourself to fall, make mistakes, understand the lessons, forgive yourself, and move on.
- Letting go of perfectionism: Accept that no one is perfect.
- Be present: Stay in the present moment to fully enjoy life and manage your emotions effectively.
- Be progressive: Embrace each small activity that helps improve and empower yourself.

## 3. Lack of awareness of your own needs

"When I bought a new phone, it worked smoothly for the first six months. Its outstanding pixel feature made me eager to capture everything and share it with my loved ones.

I installed numerous apps to assist in various areas of my life. However, after six months, it began to slow down, and by the time a year had passed, the phone would frequently hang or lose network connectivity unless it was rebooted.

The service centre explained that I hadn't been deleting messages regularly, which caused the phone's gallery to become overstuffed. Additionally, the many apps drained the battery quickly and interfered with the phone's performance.

They told me that the phone wouldn't work optimally unless all data was removed and the device was reset. So, I lost all my data and started fresh with minimal information on the phone."

Now, think of it this way: if a phone needs regular decluttering to operate smoothly, then we, as humans, whose storage capacity is far greater, also need periodic decluttering to function intelligently and serve ourselves and others happily and wisely. Unlike a phone or any other object, we are irreplaceable.

Therefore, we must be cautious and conscious of our own needs on the mental, physical, emotional, and soul levels.

Many people deny the need for self-care, thinking they can manage without it. This mindset often leads to neglecting one's well-being until they finds oneself in a complex situation.

*Imagine this:*

For a moment, close your eyes and picture yourself as a small child, crying bitterly. While your eyes are closed, look around—there are many people, but no one is there to console you. Suddenly, someone grabs your hand and starts dragging you. You cry out in pain, but that person is indifferent, pulling you away and leaving you all alone in a new place.

Now, open your eyes. Yes, that child represents your needs, your mind, body, emotions, and soul- and the person who dragged you is also you. Think deeply:-

- What are you doing to that child?
- Are you listening to your needs?
- Are you taking the time to pause and address what that child requires to be comforted?

You won't serve any purpose for yourself or your loved ones by living in denial. Ignoring your needs in any area diminishes your divine power. Research shows that this kind of neglect leads to various mental health issues.

*How to dismantle this barrier:*

- Talk to yourself first. What do I need to feel happy from within and energised sustainably?
- If necessary, talk to trusted individuals who won't judge you and can offer guidance.
- Remember, everyone is different, so what works for you should be your decision.
- With time, this will become easier, and you'll start noticing what works and what doesn't.
- Try some trial and error, but over time, you'll discover what truly works for you.
- This will make it much easier to establish your game plan, follow it, and embrace the changes for your betterment.

## 4. Guilt

Guilt is something many people feel when they try to make time for themselves. Instead of prioritising their well-being, they postpone, defer, or discard it under the pretext of other to-dos. People experience different kinds of guilt.

Some common guilt includes:

- Taking leave for relaxation only.
- Taking time away from home or kids.
- Fearing others' judgment (e.g., being seen as selfish, lazy).
- Spending spare time with friends who bring happiness.
- Spending "me time" for self-betterment.
- Spending money on self-learning, beyond family and work duties.
- Making decisions for your health without seeking family or societal approval.

*What is your guilt?*

If you resonate with anyone, then it's high time to stop feeling guilty. You might find it hard to do so, as it's deeply ingrained in our minds that self-care is selfish. Guilt often comes with negative self-talk, harsh self-judgment, and emotional distress (such as sadness, shame, anxiety, or depression).

*How to dismantle this barrier:*

- Remind yourself that you matter. You are here on Earth in a sporadic human form. Use this opportunity to the fullest to fulfil your dreams and those of your family.
- Continue to fill yourself with new knowledge and heal yourself to break free from old patterns. Grow your wings to fly, and empower your children to soar higher.

- Notice the guilt and address it gradually, inch by inch, by using healthier coping mechanisms to break free from the loop.
- Stop comparing yourself to others. Everyone is unique, and so are their needs.
- Overcome guilt by practising the following steps:
- Accept that you're feeling guilty.
- Start working on it with self-compassion (remember, you deserve care from no one else but yourself).
- Set small, achievable, sustainable goals.
- Share your intentions with your family in clear terms (this helps them understand what you're doing and eventually adjust accordingly).
- Take action with positivity and full conviction.
- If you miss your first attempt, forgive yourself and move forward with greater confidence in your second attempt.
- If you find yourself stuck, reach out for professional help.

## 5. Lack of motivation

**"Almost everything will work again if you unplug it for a few minutes, including you."**- Anne Lamott

Each of us experiences a lack of motivation in different ways at various points in our life journey. Sometimes the reasons are straightforward, while at other times they are more complex.

*Reasons for feeling a lack of motivation:*

>Too many things on the to-do list:

- When you have too many tasks on your to-do list, it can make you feel overwhelmed, which discourages you from completing them.

- This sense of being overwhelmed can push you toward procrastination

>Doubtful intentions:

- Doubt is simply a self-limiting belief.
- Self-doubt suppresses your confidence, which stops the motivation needed to take action.
- A negative attitude can ruin your motivation unless you actively work on changing it.

>Mental health issues:

- Mental health challenges, such as depression and anxiety, can prevent you from feeling motivated to take care of yourself.
- Are you upset about something?
- Are you hesitant to start a task?
- Are you feeling exhausted or overwhelmed?

>Obligatory or unrealistic goals:

- If you're doing something to please others or prove something out of ego, it won't sustain motivation.
- If your goal isn't giving you the desired push, you'll likely feel bored or disinterested.
- Without clear intentions, vague ideas about maintaining your health or achieving other goals will lead you nowhere. Your mind and body must be clear about your true intentions.

*How to dismantle the barrier:*

>Relax, sit back, take a deep breath, and calm your mind with the thought, "It's okay not to feel motivated."

>For at least one week, dedicate just 10 minutes daily to the following:

- Sit in silence near a window, in a park, in your house's lawn, or around houseplants.
- Keep your eyes open and do nothing—don't even meditate. Just observe nature.
- Feel the breeze on your face.
- Breathe normally.
- Afterwards, thank the universe and return to your daily routine.
- Through continuous observation over a fixed period, your mind will calm, brain fog will dissipate, and you will create mental space for more innovative and exciting ideas.

>Ask yourself, "What feeling is hindering my motivation?" Honour your true self-discovered reason.

>Write down what makes you feel good.

>Plan accordingly, ensuring that the actions you take give you an automatic adrenaline rush, even if it's just for 5 minutes towards your self-care, no matter how small it seems.

>After taking action, reward yourself.

>The more the action is self-oriented, the more motivation and enthusiasm you'll feel to continue performing it with fun.

>Validate each small action you take:

- "I got up on time. Wow, great job, Veenu!"
- "I brushed my teeth. Wow, great job, Veenu!"

- "I did 5 minutes of physical exercise today. Wow, great job, Veenu!"
- Self-validation, even for minor things, stacks up our happiness.
- This happiness leads to self-fulfilment.
- With self-fulfilment, you will no longer seek validation from others.

We all have moments when we feel like heroes and moments when we feel like losers. Accept each feeling with grace.

So, what if you failed or your performance was not at the desired level? There is always the next moment, the next chance. And what matters most for that next chance is that you're alive.

Only if you're alive is there a next opportunity.

- Connect happiness with valuing your life.
- Value the process of evolution through your efforts.
- Instead of tying happiness to the result, you'll find that you stop chasing happiness from one external source to the next.

**"Happiness turned to me and said, 'It is time to forgive yourself for all of the things you did not become. It is time to exonerate yourself for all of the people you couldn't save, for all of the fragile hearts you fumbled with in the dark of your confusion. It is time, child, to accept that you do not have to be who you were a year ago, that you do not have to want the same things. Above all else, it is time to believe, with reckless abandon, that you are worthy of me, for I have been waiting for years."**— Bianca Sparacino

So, accept your kingship, grab that next moment, dust off your clothes, stand tall on your past (even where you felt small, defeated, ashamed, or labelled), with more power, and smile proudly. Are you ready to love yourself?

A myth is something that has
never happened but is happening
all the time

(Joseph Campbell)

# Chapter 8 : Myths About Self-Care

"You find peace not by rearranging the circumstances of your life, but by realising who you are at the deepest level."___ Eckhart Tolle

**1. Self-care is selfish or guilty**

**Myth:**

- Thinking that self-care is a sign of vanity.
- Believing that self-care must look a particular way, such as spa days or expensive retreats, and always requires money.
- Feeling that, with family responsibilities, office targets, and kids to drop off and pick up from school/tuition/ extracurriculars, there's no time for self-care.
- Feeling guilty for doing things for your happiness while your family or children are waiting for you at home, school, or tuition.
- Worrying about what your family might say if you take time for self-care while your children are doing things like filling bottles or combing their hair on their own.
- Thinking that self-care won't put food on the table, pay bills, or meet your family's medical needs.

- Believing self-care is only for those who have house helpers.
- After working 8 hours at the office, you feel that you should take care of your family first, instead of your self-care.

*Which of these is holding you back from taking care of yourself?*

**Fact:**

- For self-care, you don't need a special environment or atmosphere (depending on the need of the hour). Self-care is done:
- When you choose to take a deep breath because you notice you're feeling stressed.
- When you give yourself three minutes before bed to sit quietly.
- When you lie in bed without gadgets, connect with your breath.
- When you talk to a friend or relative who fills you with positivity.
- When you join reunions with ex-batchmates who like you just as you are, without caring about your clothes, brands, bank balance, job, your children's achievements, or social status.
- If you experienced a difficult situation during the day, think of the opposite of it as you fall asleep to help yourself feel better inside and be grateful.
- In the beginning, your mind may tell you this won't work, or that it's silly. Acknowledge that thought and say, "Okay," then try it for two or three times. Slowly and consistently, over time, Your mind's logic will fade away.

- It will relax your tense muscles, and your body will repair and recharge whileyou sleep.

Embrace self-care as a regular practice to maintain your physical, mental, and emotional well-being.

### 2. Self-care is expensive

**Myth:**

- Thinking that self-care is only about taking a spa day, getting nails done, or shopping.
- Believing self-care is a luxury for which we have neither the time nor the money to enjoy.
- Thinking, self-care needs to take up hours of your day.
- Viewing it as a wasteful tantrum or show-off only for wealthy people who have spare money and facilities.
- Worrying that self-care will upset your budget.

**Fact:**

- Self-care is a basic human need, but it has been transformed into a commodity that people believe can only be bought with money.
- To start, identify the areas you need to improve and where it may be worth investing in yourself.
- Self-care can be as simple as sitting in nature for five minutes, smelling flowers, calling a positive friend, or serving others. Depending on your current state of mind, body, and soul, professional therapy may also be needed as part of your self-care.
- Self-care activities should be chosen based on the need of the hour. It's essential to be clear about what needs attention.

- Self-care should align with your current health condition, especially in areas that are currently causing you distress.

>**Primary Self-care:** This includes skills and techniques to help you handle or organise

your day-to-day life at home or work. Simple examples include deep breathing,

lying in bed without your phone or TV, taking a 30-minute walk, getting sound sleep,

taking a nap, playing with kids, listening to your favourite song, dancing, doing

artwork, etc.

>**Urgent Self-care:** If your mental or emotional blockages (e.g., trauma, stigma) are

disturbing your mind-body alignment, identity, or behavioural patterns, you may

need professional help for a more serious issue.

*For instance, when going to an unknown place, we use a GPS to map out our

journey, starting with small steps. Similarly, when you face a serious health or

emotional issue, start by seeking professional guidance and avoid postponing

help due to concerns about cost.

*Once your logical mind is convinced, you may realise that a single session can

make a significant difference. After that, you and the professional can decide on

the next steps as per your convenience.

**"The more you sweat in peace, the less you bleed in war."**- (Norman Schwarzkopf)

*Still doubtful?*

Here are two self-explanatory incidents that will help you:

***Incident 1 - Primary Self-care:***

"My e-office ID was fully packed with files, and I spent the entire weekend working on my laptop without a break. By the time I finished, it was 9 PM. My head started spinning, and I felt deficient. I knew it was because I had been glued to the laptop.

After dinner, I went for a long drive with my son on empty roads, playing my favourite music, and rolled down the windows to let the cool air touch my face. We stopped at a café on the way to buy hot coffee and had a heartfelt conversation. By the time I returned, I felt fully recharged."

For me, going out and enjoying the open air was the self-care I needed at that particular moment, which instantly energised and motivated me.

***Incident 2 - Urgent Self-care:***

"During the pandemic, my staff attended the office in rotation. One day, I received an urgent order at 11:30 AM from my officer to submit a file. I asked the present official, 'X,' to submit the file, but shockingly, 'X' bluntly refused, saying it was 'Y's work and that I should call 'Y' to do it.

With urgency, I sternly asked 'X' to submit the file and went into a virtual meeting. After the meeting, I found that the file was still not submitted. By 2 PM, when the file was still not on my desk, I became filled with anger, and 'X' and I had a heated argument.

After 'X' left my room, my mind started racing with fearful thoughts of all the possible adverse outcomes. My heart was pounding, anxiety set in, and I even felt that suicide might be the best option to escape the overwhelming emotions. At that moment, I almost opened the door to leave when my phone started buzzing.

By habit, I checked my phone, and it was my child calling. As soon as I answered the call, the extreme negative loop was cut off, and my mind shifted. I drank some water, called 'Y' to submit the file online, and within a short time, the issue was resolved.

However, I was still feeling suffocated and emotionally choked. Without losing time, I went to the hospital.

The doctor handled it as follows:

- He asked, 'What do you want to do NOW, in the present moment?' I cried incessantly.
- When I regained my composure, he asked me to drink water, as my body and brain were dehydrated from the stress.
- He then asked me to take a few deep breaths.
- He listened patiently to the whole scenario without speaking a word.
- He gave me a piece of paper and asked me to write 'X' and describe his behaviour.
- Then, he told me to tear the page into bits with full force and flush it down the toilet.
- He asked me to wash my hands twice with soap and feel the water flowing on them.

After completing each step, I felt like something heavy had been lifted off me.

Then, the doctor gave me two essential tips:

- Whenever you feel fearful and confused, open your mouth and breathe—breathe deeply.
- Drink as much water as you can to hydrate your mind.
- Affirm: 'If any adverse result comes, let it be. My life does not end here. I am valuable.'

- The affirmation will calm your mind first. Then, talk to someone who can help you immediately or call an emergency number to get assistance.
- Always keep some emergency contacts saved.

**3. Self-care is optional**
*Myth:*

- Self-care is something people think they can opt out of for various self-built reasons.
- "I am mentally strong, I don't have any health issues. I'm settled in my family and work life, I have a big house and a big bank account, so self-care is not my thing."
- "No one dares to fight with me, argue with me, or everyone praises me, so for me, self-care is not required."
- "What's the big deal if sometimes I have a headache or feel low?"
- "Self-care is just an emergency reaction, a crisis response."
- "I can practice self-care later."

*Fact:*

- Self-care is essential for a happy and healthy life. It is not optional, but a necessity.
- If you find yourself adopting these myth behaviours, offer yourself the attention you need directly, instead of relying on backdoor behaviours to cope.
- Neglecting your needs can lead to long-term consequences such as burnout, depression, and compulsive behaviours.
- The more you practice self-care, the easier it becomes.

- Self-care is a way to replenish your energy reserves and maintain a sense of balance.
- Instead of focusing on material things like clothes, brands, status, and achievements, value yourself by listening to your needs and being strong enough to handle failures and relationships in a more balanced and grounded manner.

### 4. Self-care is Feminine
*Myth:*

- Women bear the majority of responsibilities and handle many roles single-handedly, so self-care is seen as something only for women.
- Being sensitive, maintaining good hygiene, and taking care of yourself is considered "girly" or feminine.
- Boys and men are naturally strong and don't require as much self-care.
- Worldwide conditioning often suggests that you can only take good care of yourself after you've accomplished specific goals.

*Fact:*

- Self-care is essential for EVERYONE—regardless of gender, age, sexuality, race, or health status.
- Every person born on this Earth needs to look after their well-being.
- On the contrary, men and boys may need self-care even more, as they are conditioned from childhood to avoid crying, expressing their emotions, or sharing feelings of sadness, heartbreak, or burdens. If they do, they are labelled as "girls" or seen as weak.

- Men, especially when they are the sole breadwinners of the family, need consistent and dedicated self-care.
- Students and the elderly are more vulnerable and thus require more self-care.
- Everyone deserves and has an equal right to engage in self-care to live a happy, healthy, and positive life.

**"Self-care is holding your self-worth upright in any condition so that everything and everyone around you falls into place."**— Unknown

Caring for yourself is not Self-Indulgence, but Self-Preservation.

(Source: Google)

# Chapter 9: Self-Care Vs Self-Indulgence

**"If you do not respect your own wishes, no one else will. You will simply attract people who disrespect you as much as you do."**- Vironika Tugaleva

Most commonly, self-care is ignored by people because they think:

- Self-care is often seen as self-indulgence, and people may feel guilty about engaging in pleasurable activities.
- In both "me time" and self-care, actions are self-centric.

However, there is a vast difference between the two. The main difference is:

- Self-indulgence is a temporary moment of pleasure.
- Self-care is about taking care of yourself first to build lasting happiness, so you can also care for others with the same zeal.

> Let's break down the difference between self-care and self-indulgence further:

| Self-care | Self-indulgence |
|---|---|
| Self-Care is a Necessity, | Self-Indulgence is Temporary Gratification: |
| Self-care is rooted in the intention of promoting self-improvement and overall wellness. | temporary pleasure |
| As per one's needs on the mind, body, and soul level | Impulsive want |
| Mindful activities that nurture personal growth, resilience, and a healthier lifestyle, leading to long-term benefits. | Mindless consumption of other sources |
| Self-care activities empower us from within, which helps others also. | lead to feelings of guilt, dependency on external sources of happiness |
| Planned after reaching the root cause of the source of the need | Temporary relief to manage the symptoms without planning |
| The principle is valuing life | Valuing outer happiness or getting materialistic things. |
| Brings overall improvement | One time excitement |
| The goal is long-term well-being | No goal. (Only enjoyment that stops after a particular activity ends) |
| helps us build resilience, reduce stress, and improve our physical and mental health. | negative consequences, e.g., poor health, burn holes in pockets, or a lack of personal hygiene. |
| People doing self-care mostly enjoy being caretakers for others, besides their own care | People don't care for others' well-being |
| such as exercising, eating nutritious food, getting enough sleep, engaging in hobbies, practising mindfulness, spiritual connection, and seeking support when needed. | Such as binge-watching, binge-eating, overeating unhealthy foods, overspending on unnecessary items, or engaging in addictive behaviours. |

Though self-care and self-indulgence are two different actions, they can coexist in moderation.

However, under no circumstances should self-indulgence outweigh self-care, nor should it be an excuse to avoid responsibilities.

- For example, if you're planning dinner with your school batchmates, make sure to prepare dinner for your family before leaving. This way, you can enjoy your reunion, laugh at old jokes, and fully immerse yourself in the moment without feeling guilty.
- By making this arrangement, you'll not only enjoy the gathering, but you'll also return home with immense inner happiness.
- This inner happiness is self-care, as it becomes an immediate stimulant for your true-life force.

Take care of yourself by making wise choices in self-care, while still enjoying occasional indulgences in a balanced way with self-control and wisdom for self-preservation.

In 2015, I was invited by the University Business Studies, Punjab University, to attend the alumni meet of my M. Com batchmates in celebration of our silver jubilee. I was filled with excitement at the thought of seeing everyone after so many years.

The reunion was scheduled for the evening at 6 PM, but due to my family responsibilities, I couldn't stay out late, as there was no one else at home to care for my children and elders.

I initially decided that taking care of my family was more important than attending the reunion. With a heavy heart, I declined the invitation, promising to meet them 'next time.'

Then, one of my batchmates called and said, "Veenu! We are all lucky to have this rare opportunity to meet after 25 years. What if we don't get your 'next time' to meet again? You'll regret it for the rest of your life. Think about it and find solutions to fulfil both your responsibilities and your happiness. Take your time, and we'll respect your decision."

My "Doremon" (brain) immediately started searching for a better option, and I found a way to arrange everything smoothly for my family while I was away.

This allowed me not only to enjoy the reunion with high-pitched laughter and dancing but also to learn a great deal about education, new techniques to improve our lives, and valuable life lessons from everyone's experiences.

A key life lesson to remember:

- When you practice self-care, it fills you with eternal happiness.
- Inner happiness drives you to help others energetically and selflessly, while keeping your self-worth intact.
- Selfless care of others doesn't entangle you in an expectation loop.
- You allow others to make their own decisions, and if it's not in their best interest, you advise them with compassion, not force.
- If you take care of others without doing self-care:
- It fills you with ego, thinking you're always right and always doing things for others (especially children and spouses).
- This ego strings you into an expectation loop, where you expect others to:
- Keep you in high spirits.
- Always comply with your orders and wishes, even to the point of deciding their future.
- Praise you and show gratitude.
- When others don't recognise your efforts or take you for granted, you sulk, replaying the inner dialogue: "I'm doing everything for these people, sacrificing my needs for them, but they're so ungrateful, no one cares for

me."

- This breeds anger, frustration, fights, and eventually dampens your health with psychological and emotional issues.
- People start avoiding your company because no one wants to be around constant negativity.

Here's the question to ask yourself: *Who stopped you from being happy?*

Your inner voice is telling you the truth—it's YOU.

So, it's better to:

- First, take care of your own needs and feel your self-worth.
- Fulfil your responsibilities happily and energetically, but without expectations.
- Advise when necessary.
- This will naturally allow others to see your value and be attracted to you, just like a jasmine plant in a garden, whose fragrance is enough to guide others towards it.

**"If you want bumblebees, you don't have to chase them to collect them. Rather, grow your garden, and the bumblebees will come to you."**

- Unknown (shared by my son in one of our discussions)

Balancing is not something you

find , it is something you create.

(unknown)

# Chapter 10: Self-Care Cycle

(Source:Canva)

**"The only way to make sense out of change is to plunge into it, move with it, and join the dance."** (Alan Watts)

Self-care is like a bicycle. It runs smoothly on the bumpy roads of responsibilities, family, professional commitments, etc., only when the supporting parts are aligned.

With each part's support, it can be pedalled for the long haul.

Self-care is a restorative practice that rejuvenates and relaxes the mind, enhancing the well-being of all areas of mental, spiritual, emotional, and physical health.

Self-care works sustainably with the help of supporting wheels such as:-

- Mindfulness
- Setting Boundaries
- Resilience
- Self-compassion, self-awareness, and self-efficacy
- Humour and playfulness

Self-care practices grow you into your full, authentic self with the support of these wheels.

### A) Mindfulness

Mindfulness is the ability to be fully present in the moment, observe what you are doing, and—most importantly—what you feel and think. The goal is to remain aware of how you're feeling, whether you're experiencing low energy, burnout, or stress at any given moment.

Your mind can be like a naughty toddler; if left unchecked, it can create havoc in both your mind and body.

Instead of piling up negative emotions or succumbing to fearful thoughts, mindfulness helps you take the necessary actions to feel better. It's a health-promoting intervention.

>>Mindfulness can be practised in various ways, such as:-

>Intentional Pause: This rewires your brain, which often operates in autopilot mode. Various neural networks from old habits cause you to relapse into old behaviours before you even notice. Mindfulness slows down your brain and enables you to control your actions, willpower, and decisions, creating new and renewed neural pathways.

>Practice: I set alarms during my commute, at work, and before leaving the office to take two minutes to focus on conscious breathing or sit in silence. I also practice a technique I learned in my Health and Wellness Coaching course:

* Take three deep breaths.

* Close your eyes for five seconds.

* Become aware of your breathing.

* **Affirm:** "I am grateful to the Divine for this opportunity to connect to breath."

>> Attentive Cooking and Eating

*i) Mindful Eating-* Eating is essential for producing energy for your mind and body to work in sync.

To practice mindful eating, be attentive to what you are eating, how you are eating it, and how much you are consuming.

One of the most eye-opening lessons I learned in my Yoga certification was about mindful eating.

It taught me that:

• The emotions we experience while eating are transferred to our minds and bodies.

- Cooking food with a contaminated or negative mindset passes that unhealthy energy onto our family.
- To deepen your relationship with food, savour its texture, smell, and taste fully, free from distractions.

In the past, lunch breaks with colleagues often involved gossip about health issues, emotions, or family problems. I used to experience similar situations, but I never understood the cause. Through mindfulness, I realised that while eating, we should pay attention to what we are eating and the emotions it evokes.

After applying this practice, I began to feel more grounded in my body. Before eating, I thank God for the food and affirm: "I feel so energetic and positive with this divine food." This practice helped me improve my digestion.

### ii) Mindful Cooking

As the famous B.K. Shivani says, "Jaisa ann waisa mann, jaisa mann waisa ann," i.e, "As the food, so the mind; as the mind, so the food." The type and quality of food we consume influence our thoughts, emotions, and mental well-being.

When you cook food, your mind can throw fearful, stressful, or painful thoughts. Initially, be attentive to your thoughts. If you find yourself lost in unnecessary thoughts, immediately shift your focus and thank God for the food you're preparing.

I repeat affirmations related to my intentions, family well-being, or my children's health while cooking. This practice, surprisingly, has also improved my ability to be mindful of my listening. Now, I'm more patient and listen more attentively, both at home and at work. Initially, wandering would be frequent, but without guilt. Just come back and start what you were doing.

>> Attentive Wake-up and Sleeping Routine

*i) Wake-Up Routine*

When you wake up, it's time to reclaim your awareness and remind yourself that you deserve good things. Reaffirm your self-worth and recognise that divine powers bless you. Your smartphone doesn't have to be part of your morning routine.

Upon waking:

- Immediately express gratitude to the divine for being alive.
- If you're struggling, at least say "Good morning" to yourself, hug yourself, and express heartfelt love.
- Sit on the bed, look into your palms, and smile at yourself with deep gratitude.
- Say good morning to the divine and express thanks for your bed, the roof over your head, and anything else that comes to mind.
- Chant a mantra or affirmations according to your belief (e.g., "I am happy and grateful; I am a magnet for success in everything I do").
- If you are an atheist, place your hands on your heart, smile lovingly, and acknowledge that you are alive.
- When your feet touch the floor, express gratitude to Mother Earth for providing space for you to stand.

*ii) Sleep Routine*

Before sleeping, rewind your day and transform any negative situations into positive outcomes. Be grateful for everything good you experienced. If you feel disturbed, meditate on it to understand the root cause and ask for divine guidance to resolve it.

If you're not into meditation, focus on your breathing:

- Sit, close your eyes, and breathe in through your nose, exhaling loudly through your mouth with a forceful "haah."
- After a few breaths, breathe in and repeat, "With this breath, I invite the universe into me." Feel the cool air filling your body.
- When breathing out, mentally believe that all negative emotions are leaving your body. Repeat until you feel better, then sleep peacefully knowing you've allowed the divine to take care of you.

Apply a good-quality moisturiser or oil to your body before bed to help you relax. If I'm exhausted, I simply massage oil or ghee onto my feet, which instantly relaxes my muscles and helps me sleep deeply, waking up feeling recharged.

>>*Mindful Workout*

Whether you're cycling, going to the gym, practising yoga, jogging, or walking, being mindful during your workout makes it more effective. As you move and breathe, you release stagnant energy and uplift your mood.

While stretching or walking, stay focused on the purpose of your workout. Unplug your favourite playlist or put your phone down and be fully present in your activity. Feel your body sensations, and command your mind to focus on your breath.

Appreciate your current abilities and be thankful for your mind and body for supporting you in maintaining your physical, mental, and emotional well-being.

>>*Working Mindfulness*

With mindful presence:-

- Your attention is activated in one place.
- It increases neuronal activity as various regions of your brain are engaged.
- It decreases activity in other areas of the brain, allowing new actions to emerge.

*Key ingredients to do mindfulness: -*

- Intentional awareness of your internal experiences in the present moment.
- Allow yourself to feel the storm of thoughts without avoiding or judging them.

Mindfulness is an evolving practice; the more you practice, the more connected you'll become to your self-care.

Through the practice of mindfulness, we initiate the process of reestablishing connectedness within our bodies and strengthening our well-being with each slight movement.

"**Mindful is a way of befriending ourselves and our experiences.**" (Source: Google)

**B) Setting Boundaries**

When a house or any building is erected, the first thing done is to set boundaries.

(source:Sora)

In human life, setting boundaries is crucial for protecting your identity in every relationship, at any place you are, including within yourself.

Setting boundaries means drawing an invisible line around yourself to identify what is acceptable behaviour and what is unacceptable behaviour. In other words, you teach other people how to treat you.

To set effective and sustainable boundaries, it's very important that:-

- You are clear about your needs.
- You know how to say 'NO' sternly when needed to make people hear you.
- You do things (or take actions) that make you feel comfortable and safe.
- You feel safe to express your views.
- Your body and mind know when others are crossing their limits.
- You believe that you are a simple human being who has limits and seeks others' support when needed (from real, helping people).
- You manage your discomforts in relationships (with family members, toxic friends, relatives, etc.) or at your workplace.
- You are aware of your limits when helping others, rather than becoming a superhero; i.e., you are not dragging yourself to help others without happiness or grudgingly.

Therefore, it is crucial to communicate your boundaries.
>>**Types of Boundaries**- Healthy boundaries are set in different areas of your life-
i)*Physical boundaries*
relate to physical contact, privacy, and the body.
For example:

- You are aware of your comfort level with physical touch.
- You are aware of the safety in a particular place.
- You share your space when you feel comfortable and safe.

• You know when verbal comments on your appearance, sexuality, or anything related to your physical being are unacceptable.

**ii)** *Mental boundaries*

refer to your thoughts, values, and opinions on specific things, subjects, or decisions.

*You respect your thoughts, regardless of what another person's perspective may be.

*You share your opinions only on required matters and avoid oversharing.

*You allow others to share sensitive information only.

**iii)***Emotional Boundaries*

Emotional boundaries suggest you don't let guilt get in the way of your decisions because you recognise that you have a choice in every situation and relationship.

"In my childhood, I was very plump and short, so I was bullied many times in the playground and was called with a variety of 'names'. I would feel bad, but I didn't dare to say anything to others.

I knew only to cry or keep laughing with the children, to be part of their company. I never told this to my family either. This became part of my identity. It continued even until the second year of my graduation.

One day, one of my 'so-called friends' commented on my height. I didn't know what to say; I just laughed, and then the whole group started laughing at my "balloon" body and short height. I cried and shared this with my mother.

She told me:

• "Don't sit with people who pull you down or insult you; they are not friends."

- "Leave the company or place where you feel suffocated or unhappy. People-pleasing will not let you breathe freely."
- "First, accept your body, be it fat or short, and be thankful that whatever it might be, you are still healthy and able to do your daily routine on your own without anyone's support." (She pointed towards my paralysis-affected, bedridden grandfather, who couldn't move his body or even his tongue.)
- "This will give you the confidence to speak sternly about body-shaming."
- "Declare 'love it or leave it' to your peers to live freely without fear that they will leave you."
- "At the first instance, make your trolls very clear that they have to accept you as you are, and that their statements are hurting you and not making you feel good."
- **'Be emotional but don't be an emotional fool.'**

This teaching not only changed my perception towards my flaws but also those of others.-

iv) *Financial boundaries*

Help you organise your money to spend, save, and work for society's welfare satisfactorily.

v) *Core value boundaries*

Exist when you know what behaviours are crossing your core values—for example, lying, cheating, or double standards.

vi) *Time boundaries*

Protect your precious time by focusing on quality causes.

- You set the time for where and how much time is spent on any action.
- It helps you limit the amount of time spent listening to someone else's problems, and the same for you.
- You know when to take calls, no matter what, except in extreme circumstances.

>> *So, setting boundaries is:-*

- Knowing your worth and your uniqueness (only then will people respect you).
- Clarity of your self-respect.
- Not smiling with pained lips, say "NO" sternly and clearly to any action, invitation, occasion, or undue favours contrary to your ethical values.
- Respecting your efforts by not being readily available to sacrifice for the sake of others' comfort and happiness.

>>*How to set boundaries:*
i) *Set boundaries when you are calm, keeping in mind that:*

- You can't control how people respond to your boundaries, especially if you've never communicated them and they're not accustomed to them.
- What you can always do is stick to your boundaries, even when you feel uncomfortable.
- Be kind, and give others time to adjust to your boundaries.
- Boundaries are not meant to control others, but to protect your well-being.
- With practice, you will become comfortable with maintaining structured boundaries, and others will also come to respect you.

ii) *Create Boundaries while listening to the plight of your mind and body*

- People are wired to value what requires effort rather than what is free.
- With easy availability, some people don't respect the effort put in, but rather expect it. So, better be careful that you are-

>Offering your time, energy, values, and presence only to those who respect you.

\> Making your availability scarce to insensitive people who show up as per their convenience is not
selfishness but **self-preservation.**

\> By crushing your inner voice of discomfort, dislike, depletion, fear, frustration, or low energy, you
protect your mental peace, NO MATTER WHAT.

- Create distance, move away, or step back from toxic people.
- Treat your time, energy, and money as precious.
- Even within your family, explain your feelings and availability politely, providing proper reasons.
- It will take time, but things will improve.
- If someone in the family doesn't agree to it initially, stick to your work schedules or declarations; slowly, things will fall into place.

"After doing the YTT Course from the Bodhi School of Yoga, Hyderabad, in August 2023, I started teaching Yoga in September 2023. I, being a working mother of two studying sons, and my first student (being a homemaker), fixed the time at 7:30 PM as that was mostly our free time, in between evening tea and dinner. Happily, I shared with my family that from the next day, I would start teaching Yoga at 7:30 PM.

After a few days of smooth running, one of our relatives (from my in-laws' side) came to stay with us for a few days at 7 PM due to some office work.

I served tea and opened the link to join the Yoga class. At 7:40 PM, my son called me to cook dinner for his uncle, as he was in the habit of having dinner at 7:45 PM and going to sleep by 8 PM.

I said sorry to my student and ended the class abruptly. This repeated for the next day as well.

When I discussed with my family that cooking dinner at 7:45 PM was disrupting my routine, they convinced me that in 3-4 days, he would leave, so it would be better to serve him food at his convenience. This forced duty was making me feel more helpless, elevating my anger and stress, as I was unable to keep my word to my student.

One day, I gathered my courage, and at 6:30 PM, when my whole family was sitting in the guest room with my uncle, I served tea and, in between, told them that I am a Certified Yoga teacher and teach Yoga online.

He appreciated my efforts and asked when I would be teaching yoga. I quickly replied, "From 7:30 PM to 8:30 PM, so I cook dinner at 8:35 PM.

To my surprise, on that day, no one called me in between to cook dinner for my uncle, and my class started and ended at the fixed time peacefully.

With my polite but straightforward and respectful words, I genuinely created respect in Uncle's eyes for my work."

> If toxic people are there in the family or work:-

- Politely refuse to be their emotional support backup.
- Humbly express your emotions to make them realise.
- Don't dim your light even if such a person resents or disappears the moment you say a clear "NO." Let that person go and stay in your absence.
- If someone creates scenes or makes you fearful of walking your path, be stable, leap higher, and let them be uncomfortable with your growth.

> By choosing unhealthy options over setting boundaries, you will:-

- Complain more (whenever you get the chance).
- Avoid expressing your opinions or discomfort.
- Reluctantly use pacifying statements like "I will sell," "I will tell you," "Let me think," instead of saying a clear and stern "NO" to anything that goes against your moral values or righteousness of cause.
- Be nothing more than a ladder for others to reach their highest and fulfil their dreams.
- Be used by people as a trash box for venting or ruminating rather than seeking sincere guidance, as they don't think you're capable enough to help them.
- Take responsibility for fixing other people's emotions while also working on your own.
- Cut yourself loose from spiritual commitments. In our religious prayers, we commit to God to obey His orders, but in reality, we do what others decide for us and forget to fulfill what the Creator intended for us when He created us.
- Eventually, you move away from your true self-worth and self-calibre and become blind to parts of yourself you're not willing to face.

Everyone's set of boundaries will be different, as we all have distinct thinking patterns, likes, and situations. So, our boundaries cannot be the same.

>> *Boundaries can be communicated in two significant ways:-*

*Verbally-*

- Through a stern and straightforward declaration, let others know that you don't like, feel

uncomfortable with, or find a specific action morally wrong.

*Action-*

- By not doing things you are unsure about.
- By not doing things that make you uncomfortable.
- By not doing things that make you feel doubtful or unsafe.
- By not doing or sharing something that crosses your privacy.
- Keep your personal and professional life separate.
- Don't take calls at odd hours or when it's inconvenient for you.

>>*How to maintain boundaries*

1. There will be people around you, especially those in power, who may want you to stay small or doubt your divine virtues or real worth. But stay calm and don't be ashamed of your boundaries.
2. Don't bend your boundaries to please indifferent people or society (like I did).

3.  Don't bend them out of fear that someone might leave you.
4.  In these situations, saying 'NO' is the best form of self-care.
5.  Everyone is different, so will your boundaries be.
6.  Check your boundaries daily and refrain from taking actions that contradict your principles, especially in the workplace.
7.  Keep taking small steps, and over time, you'll create success stories to share with others.

*How have you set your boundaries:-*

- When was the last time you achieved something with your calibre?
- When was the last time you did something solely for your pleasure?
- When was the last time you tried something for the first time, felt proud of yourself, and felt on cloud nine?

**"In your life, you are not the issue. Maybe the whole world is the issue."** - Sadhguru

C) Resilience

Resilience is derived from Latin, where re means "back" (again) and salire means "to leap." Resilience is a person's ability not only to survive the jarring setbacks but also to bounce back.

The setbacks can stem from stress, personal patterns, complex relationships, health issues, or significant events like the death of a loved one, natural calamities, divorce, or financial struggles.

Resilience is a skill that you develop, which reinforces your inner strength by changing your mindset, all while keeping one thing in mind: "Life is unpredictable."

To tackle the unexpected, you need to be open to new changes and experiences, and adapt to them as opportunities for learning. (Neenan, 2018)

>> *Importance of Resilience*

When you start focusing on self-care, challenges will always be there. The challenge may be something significant or even something as simple as procrastination. Sometimes, challenges come in the form of family criticism or a lack of cooperation, and professional life, some difficult people may try to bring you down.

However, whatever situation comes your way, the skill of resilience will help you find a way to overcome it differently, utilising your capacity. Like other skills, consistent work is required to develop your resilience muscle.

Your challenge may be so drastic that you are emotionally broken-

- Don't suppress emotion; accept whatever you are feeling.
- Allow yourself to feel low. We are human, so it's natural to feel sad or cry.
- Take your time to heal yourself with kindness.

>> How to Grow Resilience

**i)** Focus more on solutions than problems.

- With practice, start with small things-
- First, analyse the situation that is bothering you.
- Think of as many options as you can to solve it.
- Please choose the most effective solution and work on it.

## ii) Consistency

- Start by working consistently on one or two things.
- This increases the success rate, builds confidence, and gives a sense of accomplishment, which contributes to resilience.

## iii) Expressing your views

- Improve self-awareness to understand your thoughts, emotions, and behaviours in a situation to respond effectively.
- Whenever you hear negative thoughts in your mind, immediately replace them with positive self-talk.
- Only then will you be able to respond more positively and effectively.
- Learn to express your needs and feelings clearly and assertively.
- At the same time, actively listen to others.

## iv) Relaxation techniques

- Learn relaxation techniques such as deep breathing, meditation, or playing an instrument.
- Keep a record of activities in advance that serve as references whenever needed, rather than relying on others for help all the time.

## v) Coping mechanism

- Embrace change, as it is inevitable.
- Only when you accept it will your mind stop terrifying you with extreme, adverse outcomes and a lack of hope.

- Acceptance will quiet your mind's chattering, and as soon as you restore calmness, your mind will bring a ray of light through some idea of hope.
- Deal with it from a positive perspective-

1. Keep the belief that there is always a solution to any situation, and also believe in

your abilities and inbuilt strengths.

2. This belief will help you gather the courage to take action toward the solution

3. Your efforts, combined with a belief in hope, will naturally manifest the right

people and opportunities to support you in overcoming the challenge.

- Naturally, sometimes you may fall into negative self-talk and lose hope or courage to continue turning the situation in your favour. In such times, intentionally start positive self-talk mentally and also write down things you're grateful for by focusing on the good things still present in your life.
- Remember! Just as you might have learned religious scriptures, songs, verses, or mantras through repeated practice, similarly, keep repeating positive thoughts or self-talk with patience. Have faith that your ability to cope with hardship with grace is becoming stronger and stronger.

>>*Divine Connection*

- It is natural that when any challenge or situation hits you hard, you may lose your divine connection, thinking that God has punished you or your loved ones for some curse unnecessarily.

- Accept your feelings and listen to all your inner thoughts. You have every right to feel this way; it's a genuine concern. Even then, believe that you are God's child, so you deserve the opportunity to complain to God. Like children, surrender this situation to Him and ask Him to handle it.

- Once you connect to God, slowly this will give you solace and hope, knowing that someone will set everything right. If not everything, then something better will come your way.

- For those who are sceptical, divine guidance can be sought through meditation or simply being in nature. It is a feeling of peace, love, and understanding that comes from a deep place within.

- Engaging in mindfulness practices, such as meditation, provides you with lessons from each situation (no matter how adverse it is or how far it has uprooted you). It brings a new purpose to life, encouraging you to take care of yourself, resulting in improved mental health. In time, you'll stand firm on your past. Keep practising and make yourself like smiley balls, no matter how hard one tries to suppress them, once released, they bounce back swiftly with a proud smile.

**"Resilience is not what happens to you. It's how you react to, respond to, and recover from what happens to you."**- Jeffrey Gitomer

**d) Self-compassion, Self-awareness, and Self-efficacy**
For sustainable self-care, you need:

- I) Self-compassion
- II) Self-awareness

- III) Self-efficacy

### I) Self-compassion

- Self-compassion means being supportive to yourself when you're facing a life challenge and feel inadequate.
- Instead of ignoring your pain or getting carried away by negative thoughts and emotions, you tell yourself, "This is difficult right now. How can I comfort and care for myself in this moment?"
- Whenever needed, allow yourself to be helped in the form of a hug or sincere advice from your loved ones. Sometimes, you need that support.
- Self-care with self-compassion aligns you with your needs, decisions, and improved self-talk.
- Self-compassion becomes more powerful when you acknowledge your vulnerabilities with kindness,
- rather than hiding them or being blind to them.

>>*How to practice self-compassion:*

- Befriend yourself with your ethical values.
- Take regular breaks in between your busy schedule.
- Before going to sleep, note your feelings.
- Sit in meditation and keep an observational approach.
- Be open to experiencing the full range of human emotions, honour them without suppression, exaggeration, or avoidance.
- Release the feelings with loving affirmations, self-talk, or blessings for yourself.
- Use affirmations to increase love and kindness for yourself.

- Daily, refill yourself with your belief in your divinely blessed strengths and abilities.
- Be grateful to God or anything you believe in as a higher power or the universe.

## II) Self-awareness / Self-evaluation

Self-awareness means staying attuned to both your strengths and areas for growth in your thoughts and overall being.

It is the ability to see yourself clearly and objectively through reflection and introspection without judgment.

Only with this awareness can you motivate yourself and take personal responsibility to make the specific changes needed for a given reason. Self-compassion enhances your self-determination.

It becomes the biggest tool to strengthen acceptance and readiness to work on improving any shortcomings, instead of sweeping them under the carpet. Self-awareness teaches you to be aware of your thoughts and actions.

One of my friends was struggling to clear his promotion exam within the given schedule, despite being intelligent. Most of his juniors passed the exam, which made him feel very embarrassed about the situation.

When he shared this with me and sought my help, I asked him to analyse his behaviour and thoughts during the exam and reflect on what disturbed him before and during the test.

He asked himself what made the task so hard for him, and after introspection, he realised that it wasn't negative thoughts holding him back. Instead, he was not writing his answers clearly and cohesively.

He then decided to address this by taking a course to improve his writing ability, focusing on presenting balanced and relevant information more systematically and effectively.

**III) Self-efficacy**

Self-efficacy refers to the belief that you can accomplish something. Three factors influence self-efficacy

- Personal
- Environmental
- Behavioural

Self-efficacy is the foundation stone for every step toward achieving sustainable self-care.

The more you instill belief in your capacity to do anything, the closer you will get to your goal of becoming the version of yourself that you desire.

*Affirmations* (such as "I am powerful," "I am the co-creator of my life," etc.) are among the most effective tools for improving self-efficacy.

**"Self-efficacy is the belief in one's capabilities to organize and execute the sources of action required to manage prospective situations."**-(Source:Google)

**D) Humour and Playfulness**

Consistent seriousness can drain you and hinder your progress.

The more you laugh and see the lighter side of your challenges, the more opportunities you'll find to open yourself up to change.

Playfulness fuels your energy, enabling you to work effectively with zest and connect to life in a more meaningful way. Learn to laugh at your mistakes along the way.

Compared to children, adults seldom get time to play, so keeping your joy and sense of humour alive is crucial for feeling refreshed and rejuvenated.

**"Don't take yourself too seriously, but extraordinarily perform your work.** (A joyful Coach in my health and wellness coaching)

• 145 •

Almost everything will work again
if you unplug it for a few minutes,
including you

(Anne-Lamont)

# Chapter 11: Types of Self-Care

"**Self-care is an attitude that says I am responsible for myself.**" - Melody Beattie

Engaging in activities that promote self-care through internal work is a valuable approach.

In other words, whatever you decide to do should be done with a purpose, not influenced by someone else.

For sustainable self-care, it's essential to be clear about how you're feeling and which self-care practice will soothe you.

For example:-

- Sometimes you need breathing exercises.
- Sometimes you need to cook a special meal.
- Sometimes you need to say 'NO' to any engagement.
- Sometimes you need alone time.

In other words, Responsibility means- "I am" my responsibility.

- Responsibility is response + ability, meaning the ability to respond.

It means being sure that whatever you are doing is based on your own needs, not because others like it or because others are doing it.

And you will honour that responsibility more than anything else precious to you. This responsibility requires you to be in tune with your higher self, and that connection comes by practising self-care at different levels.

# Types of self-care
a) Mindset (psychological) self-care
b) Emotional self-care
c) Physical self-care
d) Workplace self-care
e) Spiritual self-care
f) Social self-care
g) Environmental self-care

***a) Psychological (Mindset) Self-care***

**"Most problems we face in life happen in our minds."**
- (Anonymous)

WHO defines mental health as:

- "A state of mental well-being that enables people to cope with the stresses of life, realise their abilities, learn well and work well, and contribute to their community."

In simple words, psychological (mindset) self-care is about cultivating a healthy mindset through various practices, so you can:-

- Think clearly when experiencing something unexpected or unfavourable.
- Analyse things critically.
- Enhance learning ability.

- Update your knowledge to improve your own and others' lives.

>>*Mental self-care helps you to:*

- Develop coping mechanisms to manage stress, anxiety, and burnout.
- Guide you to take the desired or required action in the right direction.
- Lower the risk of illness or help cure a disease.
- Increase energy, resilience, and perseverance.
- Maintain the body's health.
- Make better decisions in any situation.
- Take the first step to bounce back from any adverse situation.

>>*Factors Impacting Mindset Health:*

- Family: e.g., genes, sleep, age.
- Community connection: e.g,. culture, work, friends, support system.
- Structural factors: e.g., people exposed to adverse circumstances (poverty, violence, disability, inequality) are at a higher risk of developing mental health conditions.
- Water intake, Diet
- Involvement of the mind in learning: e.g., how do you keep your mind updated with knowledge? How do you keep your mind busy?
- Wiring of your mind: whether it's a positive or negative mindset.

>> How to Analyse Your Mental Health

- A few simple self-questioning techniques will help you analyse your mental health:
- What beliefs do you have for yourself?
- Rate from 1-10 your good memories and painful memories.
- Do you enjoy being with yourself?
- Do you need people to feel happy?
- When was the last time you overcame a challenging situation with a positive mindset?

*Even if the answers present a not-so-good picture, still accept the reality, as acceptance is the entry gate

to the house of your true happiness.

* Now, proceed to the detailed questionnaire in Chapter 5 for Mindset Health.

The questionnaire in Chapter 5 will make it crystal clear if you need meditation, nature connection,

* clinical support, or therapeutic help. After completing the Q&A, you will be able to assess whether you

are psychologically healthy or if you need to do some work to take care of yourself.

| Mentally healthy if | Need to take care if |
|---|---|
| Positive outlook toward self, | Negative outlook toward self |
| Focus more on solving difficult situations | Avoid the difficult situation |
| Feel self-confident in the existing environment | Feel an inadequate environment or a misfit |
| Have techniques to cope with stress, anxiety, etc. | Stay entangled in the loop of low-level thoughts rather than acting. |
| Able to decide something on their own. | Rely on others for decisions |
| Enjoy the relations (of family, friends, or at work) in life | Grudges/complaints in Problematic, disturbed relations (of family, friends, or at work) |
| Accept the responsibility with self-confidence | Avoid the responsibility (thinking you will not be able to do it correctly) |
| Can work independently | Need people's help to do the work |
| Easy adaptation with changed situations in life (as change is inevitable in life) and | It is difficult to accept the changes in life |
| find happiness in anything | Very selective to be happy |
| easily ask for help (from better-guided people) if needed, and accept | Feel shy/reluctant to seek anyone's help if needed |
| Have a good sense of humour | They like to stay in their shell |
| Your body is healthy, and if a disease happens, you know how to cure it with the support of a positive mindset along with medicines. | As the mind and body are interconnected, your body might be facing some mild or acute diseases. |

>> *How to Strengthen Psychological Self-care:*
i) To bring your focus to the present moment:

- Practice meditation, yoga, muscle relaxation, or breathing exercises.

ii) To uplift your esteem from feelings of low, sadness, or "Why me?"

- Count your blessings.
- Walk in nature, along trees.
- Look into the sky, observe it, and see the stars.

iii) To strengthen your mental power:

- Participate in creative activities you enjoy.
- Read good books on mind health, such as my all-time favourite, 'Heal Your Body' by Louise Hay.
- Engage in games such as Scrabble, crossword puzzles, or other brain teasers and mental exercises.
- Engage in additional breathing exercises, such as conscious breathing, Anulom-Vilom, and Bhastrika.

> conscious breathing (source: Google)???
*Place your hands as shown in the image.
*Close eyes (optional), naturally breathe in and out, yet focus on speed,
*Temperature of breath
*Set the time at your convenience.
> anulom vilom
*Keep right hand's thumb on right nostril, ring finger on left nostril very gently.
*Fold the index finger and middle finger towards the right palm.
* Lift ring finger, inhale from left nostril, hold the breath and close the nostril again

*Lift your thumb and exhale through your right nostril.

*Now inhale through the right and exhale through the left as cited above.

*First, repeat the process at your convenience.

*End the process with exhalation from the left.

> bhastrika (bellows breathing) -

* Inhale, and stretch your arms up over your head.

*Make the fist.

*Exhale with force while bringing your arms down next to your rib cage.

*Start with a slow speed at your pace and when learnt the process, begin rapid inhalation and

exhalation.

* Set a time that suits your convenience and learning style.

iv) To clear doubts about any mind behaviour:

• Seek help from a professional as needed.

* To improve your body's health, you have to be mentally strong. In this process, prepare a coping

mechanisms in advance to easily untangle yourself from emotional stirs as early as possible:

• Either remove completely or at least minimise fear/ anxiety.
• Channel low esteem to high self-esteem.
• Protect self-respect/self-connection.
• Be your authentic self, your truest and happiest self.

***b) Emotional Self-care***

When you cross someone known to you, the first question you casually repeat is "How

Are you?"

- Did you ever sincerely ask yourself this question?
- Did you ever notice emotions brewing, overflowing, or whistling within you, waiting for you to listen?

If you haven't until now, be a good listener to your feelings and be emotionally healthy,
too. Emotional health is the ability to accept, understand, and navigate your emotions to
live effectively through challenges and change.
In simple words, an individual can:-

- Handle stress and emotional challenges.
- Heal yourself when faced with difficult times and thrive overall.
- Focus more on being authentically vulnerable.

>**Myth:** Good emotional health means an individual has to always be happy or free from negative emotions.
>**Fact:** An emotionally healthy person is someone who is happy primarily but is always aware of their feelings, understands their root causes, analyses the reasons, and resolves them with the skills and resources available to manage the ups and downs of daily life.
If something not-so-good or extreme happens in their life, they allow themselves to feel low or broken, as they are human, and pain will be there, at a loss. But, after a certain point, an emotionally healthy person will dust off, make sense of the situation, and start focusing on what they can change, rather than dwelling on what has been lost. If needed, they will provide adequate help.
Factors impacting emotional health:-

- Challenges at work or school.
- Changes in health.
- Difficult relationships.
- Retirement.
- Social connections.
- Sudden life changes.
- Lost connection with the supreme power/highest good.

>>Analysing Emotional Health

1) Refer to the detailed questionnaire provided in Chapter 4 for information on emotional health.

- The questionnaire in Chapter 4 will make it crystal clear the status of your emotional health.
- After completing the Q&A, you will be able to analyse your emotional health status.

| Emotionally healthy if | Need to charge up if |
| --- | --- |
| Like self-company and good rapport with others | Isolating from friends, family, or co-workers |
| Sound and adequate sleep | Disturbed sleeps |
| Mostly high energy. but anyhow, if the energy level drops, sort it out with already set inner tools. | Low energy/ exhaustion |
| Sound sleep | Disturbed sleep/insomnia |
| Quality or balanced diet. | Inadequate eating pattern |
| High performance | Lower performance at work |
| Awareness of thoughts | Inattentive towards thoughts |
| Resilience | stress/ irritation/ guilt, hopelessness, or worthlessness, causing physical illness |

II) Deeper work on emotions can be done through the emotional wheel as described in Chapter 6

>>How to Strengthen Emotional Self-care

- Accept the emotions honestly and then plan your next course of action.
- Surround yourself with supportive, positive people.

- Look inward for validation, not outward.
- Keep a check and intentionally avoid negative self-talk throughout the day.
- Make time for the things you enjoy, regardless of age, societal expectations, or a busy schedule.
- Focus more on doing things rather than the length of time. (You must have heard, "something is better than nothing").
- If needed, seek professional help (rather than living in denial).
- Stay connected to the higher power in your powerless situations. You are like a smartphone that needs to be charged daily. Through prayer, or however you choose to accept it, recharge your energy twice a day to work smoothly.
- Listen to triggers:-

*When you attract the same kind of difficult people, situations, or patterns that evoke the same

*Emotions it is a sign that something is unresolved or unhealed within you.

*Accept and look into the trigger, embrace it, notice it, and its pattern.

*Noticing and healing is the solution or tool for you to change your situation in your favour.

*No one else is bothered enough to do it for you.

*Be your healer with love, and be grateful to your triggers for giving you direction to be whole and complete.

Prepare some uplifting statements (as illustrated below) and repeat them at your convenient pace during the day, especially before bedtime and first thing in the morning.

Place your hand on your heart and repeat:-

- I love myself wherever I am and however I am.
- I am capable of changing situations in my favour.
- I always attract the right people and right situations in my life.
- I am ready to enter into new possibilities.
- I am breaking free from my past.
- I invite God to enter into this situation with me to create magic for me.
- I am a blessed child of God.

>>Get enough sleep.

- Sleep is essential for your cells to function correctly and facilitate transformation and change in your situation, with the assistance of your affirmations.

>>Any physical movement.

- For me, leisurely nature work in my society compound acts as an immediate stress buster, breaking the loop of negative thoughts and providing a gap for the mind to breathe, oxygenate, and think more clearly.

### c) Physical Self-care

Physical self-care means taking care of your body.

It involves activities that engage your body, including muscle and core activation, and consuming foods that promote or maintain your body's health and wellness.

Physical self-care should be tailored to your body's specific needs. It needs to be flexible, realistic, and consistent, rather than following methods derived from others.

Physical Self-care helps you to experience:-

- Improved energy
- Improved productivity
- Better emotional management
- Healthy life expectancy
- Disease prevention

>>*Factors impacting physical health:-*

- Income and social status
- Education
- Environment (water, air, plants)
- Workplaces, employment, and working conditions
- Family condition
- Social support
- Customs, traditions, and beliefs of the family and community
- Genetics
- Personal behaviour (balanced eating, emotional and spiritual well-being)

>>*Analysing Physical Health:*
Besides analysing your physical health as given in Chapter 4, you also have to keep track
of your health through:

- Medical tests
- Vital measurements
- All major systems of the body (e.g., cardio/respiratory/ muscles)
- Comfort of movements in the body

>> *How to Strengthen Physical Self-care:*

- Engage in physical activity as per your body's needs.
- Eat healthy, homely, seasonal foods and fruits.
- Sometimes (especially in free time or during the day), practice mindful eating:

    * Keep your phone aside or move away from the TV.
    * Don't eat just for the sake of it.
    * Observe the food on your plate, be grateful to the divine for it, appreciate the person who cooked
    it, and acknowledge those who grew it.
    * Smell the aroma, taste the flavour, and relish the moment.


- Keep your body hydrated.
- Break the monotony of the same physical activity each day (e.g., choose a nature walk, aerobics, dance movements, or play any game you like most).
- Exercise with someone similar to enjoy more and avoid boredom, or play with children.
- Maintain a healthy, balanced weight (use stairs more than lifts/elevators).
- Don't ignore body signals.
- Sleep well.


### d) Workplace Self-care

Workplace self-care refers to intentional actions taken to maintain or improve one's physical, mental, and emotional well-being, even in the workplace.

>>Workplace Self-care helps:-

- Make work more interesting and inspirational, which automatically improves job performance.
- Increase job satisfaction.
- Combat feelings of stress or burnout.

>> *Analysing Workplace Self-care*
Firstly, ask yourself:

- Do you feel like going to the office, or are you dragging your feet?
- Do you feel like getting dressed up for the office?
- What is your happiness, satisfaction, and peace quotient at the workplace?

Then, conduct a deeper examination of workplace self-care, as outlined in Chapter 4.
>> *How to Strengthen Workplace Self-care:-*

- Set boundaries with coworkers and seniors.
- Learn to say a stern but polite NO (if you are not comfortable doing a particular task or working in a specific place that you feel is unsafe).
- Set the environment around you to inspire and uplift you, such as with plants, affirmations, or inspirational verses.
- Take breaks in between. Ditch the chair, stretch a bit, or take a stroll.
- Rest, be mindful.
- Keep hydrated.
- Laugh and engage in light-hearted conversations with coworkers.
- Ask for help whenever you need it and stand up for yourself.

- Keep professional and personal life separate.

### e) Spiritual Self-care

Spiritual self-care involves establishing a connection with one's higher or true self to keep fear, ego, and self-limiting beliefs at bay, as these are false realities.

Spiritual Self-care promotes:-

- While moving through daily real and constantly changing situations in life, it's natural to feel unwell or experience physical and mental distress, even if you are in perfect health. In these situations, spiritual practice works like recharging a house, providing clarity and comfort with balanced emotional well-being.
- Numerous health benefits arise from daily practice, as it quiets the mind and calms internal turbulence, creating space within.
- Helps you feel and honour the desires of your heart, giving you the strength to make necessary changes for the betterment of yourself and others.
- Helps you gain, maintain, or regain insight into your inner happiness.
- Enhances feelings of oneness and universality, making you feel safe and secure.
- Reduces feelings of loneliness and isolation.
- Strengthens your bond with yourself.
- With the feeling of connection to a higher power (God/ Universe), you start becoming the co-creator of your life.

*>> Factors impacting spiritual self-care:-*

- Commitment to connect.

- Desperation to bring change to the inner and outer world.
- Desire to feel genuine happiness, where your body sways in eternal joy without reason.

*>>Analysing Spiritual Health:*

- How valuable do you think having a sense of connection to something greater than yourself is?
- What is your relationship with yourself?
- Have you ever felt that spiritual self-care benefited you?
- Do you enjoy nature, just observing the sunshine, moon, stars, clouds, or birds?
- Have you experienced any magical results after connecting spiritually?
- Do you know what your spirit needs, more or less?

*>> How to Strengthen Spiritual Self-care:-*

- Meditation
- Prayer
- Yoga
- Gratitude journaling
- Serve others selflessly (in a balanced way without harming your inner peace)
- Observe and enjoy the beauty of nature around you.

### *f) Social Self-care - Basic Human Need*

Social self-care involves taking care of one's own well-being by developing and maintaining meaningful, positive social relationships, nurturing healthy relationships with family, friends, coworkers, and neighbours, and expanding one's happiness circle while avoiding toxic relationships.

Social Self-care is essential to:-

- Encourage social interactions, talk, seek help, and advice when needed.
- Offer support during challenging times and improve your overall well-being.
- Learn new things, update your knowledge, and keep your mind active and full with good information.
- After venturing into jobs and real-life ups and downs, you need someone to interact with without the stress of being judged.
- Break the dullness in life by enjoying vacations with family.
- Add spark to the monotony of life. When you are a parent of any age, you absolutely need a circle of like-minded people to talk about anything (but not gossip), laugh loudly, and do fun-filled, silly things.
- As a mother of two grown-up children, I have ample free time, which I utilise to catch up with my M.Com batch mates frequently, celebrate their achievements, or party with my very special friends, allowing me to lose all my etiquette and enjoy the genuine moments, cherishing them forever.
- Protect you from various side effects of social isolation, such as higher rates of heart disease, hypertension, diabetes, depression, anxiety, suicidal tendencies, and violence, due to less time for heart-to-heart conversations, today's sedentary lifestyle and the constant. The presence of technical gadgets pushes most people towards loneliness, even if they live in a comfortable house with family.

*>>Factors impacting social self-care:*

- Nature- Introvert/Extrovert
- Family commitments

>> Analysing Social Self-care:
Reply honestly:

- Who is living next door?
- List five names that you think are your support at any time.
- When was the last time you laughed from the heart with friends?
- When was the last time you did something silly for fun?
- When was the last time you saw children playing?
- When was the last time you talked to your neighbours?
- When did you travel last?
- When was the last time you sat with your ageing parents and talked to them, enjoying family time together?
- When was the last time you spoke to relatives or friends?

*If, after answering these questions, you find it difficult to remember, this serves as a reminder to
strengthen this connection and decrease social isolation.
*Incorporating social self-care into your routine can help you feel more balanced and supported, even
during the busiest times.
>>*How to Strengthen Social Self-care:*

- Participate in local activities.
- Plan a picnic in the park.
- Host a family reunion.
- Take a stroll in the park.
- See children playing and laughing.

- Chat with neighbours.
- Invite friends over for dinner.
- Call someone you haven't talked to in a while.
- Go on vacations.
- Plan an outing with friends.
- Join an online class.
- Grow your community of like-minded people.

### g) Environmental Self-care

Environmental self-care not only benefits the planet but also promotes a sense of well-being and connectedness with one's community. 'Environ' means surroundings, and it is clear that the environment plays a crucial role in our inner health. Thus, environmental health is essential for maintaining overall well-being.

Environmental self-care involves being mindful of the environmental conditions that impact our lives, such as reducing waste, utilising sustainable products, and participating in community cleanup efforts. Each small action contributes to creating a healthier environment.

In simple terms, environmental self-care refers to maintaining a sustainable lifestyle that balances personal health with ecological well-being.

>> *Environmental Self-care is essential to:-*

- Provide a source of inspiration, creativity, and awe, which adds meaning and fulfilment to your life.
- Preserve nature to live a comfortable life.
- Strengthen the bond with nature.
- Conserve inner energy and environmental energy.
- Meditate more peacefully with better surroundings.

>>*Factors impacting environmental self-care:*

- Natural resources
- Geography
- Technology
- Urbanization
- Globalization
- Social norms

>> How to Strengthen Environmental Self-care:-

- Use reusable shopping bags instead of plastic.
- Compost kitchen waste, use more stainless utensils and containers instead of plastic.
- Opt for Eco-friendly products, and avoid throwing garbage in open poly bags.
- Create better surroundings in your home and office by decluttering and personalising your workspace with more plants.
- On a community level, gift plants instead of other gifts, plant more trees in open spaces, keep your house (both inside and outside) greener, and maintain birdhouses.
- Use water wisely to contribute to a healthier environment.

Self care is one of the active ways that you love yourself the most and unconditionally. Make time and space in melting down moments, tiredness , and even to add happiness, do what you can, in the ways that fill you with compassion for you, clarity and inner peace.

**"Close the old history, now open a new page."** (unknown)

The only way to become excellent
is to be endlessly fascinated by
doing the same thing over and
over. You have to fall in love with
boredom.

# Chapter 12: Self-Care Techniques

a)Self-Care – Daily

b) Self-Care – Emergency or any sudden stressful situation.

c) Self-care – Extremely busy

> **a) Self-care- daily**

Self-care techniques vary from person to person. One size does not fit everyone. It must be tailored according to one's family commitments, job nature, workload, circumstances, surroundings, etc.

Self-care techniques are generally the same; what differs from person to person is the time or variation in techniques.

I, being a working woman in a nine-to-five job and a yoga teacher, have to keep my self-care techniques on working days as per my time availability. It is different on off days, so I can balance my family commitments, professional commitments, and personal commitments to recharge my energy battery through self-care.

My daily self-care techniques:-

- On working days (Monday-Friday):

i) Morning:

- Waking up early to meditate, connect to a higher power to fill my mind and body with his power, strength, and chant any mantra, express gratitude to earth/air/water, etc.
- 5-minute (at least 30 minutes on weekends or holidays) affirmation to connect my mind and body, reminding them of their divine powers and aligning them with the universe.
- Do a 5-10 min yoga practice (one hour on weekends or on holidays).
- Have breakfast (paratha or poha, porridge, cheela, etc.).
- In the office, take time to take breaks from the computer, ditch the chair.
- Hydrate as much as possible.

ii) Evening:

- 30 min family time.
- Water the plants.
- Do stretching while teaching yoga to students.
- Read a book or take a walk in nature to breathe in the fresh air.
- Do something just for your fun (e.g., listen to a song of my choice).
- Meditate and journal at least 3-5 blessings during the day.
- Self-reflect on any unhappy situation, write it down, learn a lesson from it, and intentionally turn the negative into a positive to break the loop of stress and feel happier.

- Moisturise your body with lotion or oil, and also with blessings.
- Sleep with sending blessings to oneself and repeating affirmations (at least thrice).

o "All is well, everything is working out for my highest good. Out of this situation, only

good will come, I am safe."

o "Everything is done easily and effortlessly."

o (....Your name), I behold you with eyes of love, you are God's blessed child, and God

loves you. I send you the blessings that all the goodness and success that you desire come into your

life. I also send you the blessing of health and well-being."

o "Everywhere I and my family are taken care of by the divine. My family and I are blessed children

of God."

Out of the above, you can adjust the activity and time limits according to your specific conditions or situation.

> On off days (weekends/holidays/leaves/vacations):

- Wake up half an hour earlier than on working days.
- Spend some extra time with self-affirmations, blessings, and prayers for my highest good in all levels of life.
- Stand in the space outside my room, breathe in the fresh air, and spend some time expressing gratitude for the universe, nature, and Mother Earth.
- Practice yoga sadhana for at least 40 minutes (or 1 hour).
- Practice Reiki for self-healing, empowerment, and sending Reiki healing to the world as a gesture of gratitude.

- After household chores, take naps or do whatever enhances my peace, such as book reading, gardening, writing, going to the market for essentials, pampering myself (but with wisdom), etc.
- Make sure to attend weekly online classes on self-grooming, updates, or new learnings in subjects of interest, such as writing, yoga, Reiki, meditation, dance, and emerging modalities of healing.
- The evening is devoted to my family commitments.
- Engage in extensive meditation to connect with my higher self, engage in soul talk, self-talk, and self-body awareness.
- Say prayers for the optimal growth of family members in all aspects of life.

**b) Self-Care – In emergencies or any sudden, stressful situation.**

Not all days are good days. Life brings sudden panic attacks, intense mood swings, and challenging days filled with stress and anxiety. Therefore, it's essential to have a coping mechanism ready to tackle any such situation.

It happens to me as well when I find myself struggling to breathe and regain mental and physical alignment during these stressful moments. However, with practice, my "tools" are always prepared in advance, just like having a nebuliser ready in case of respiratory distress to ensure adequate oxygen supply for my mind to function better.

For example:

- Quick, doable breathing exercise: Inhale deeply through your nose and exhale through your mouth.
- Grab water immediately (even if you don't feel like it or think you don't need it): This has been a miraculous

healer for me. The more water I drink, the more toxins I flush out, giving my mind space to inhale oxygen, which gradually clears the brain fog.

- Asanas to release stress: If possible, I sit or stand in calming poses, such as Balasana (Child's Pose), Progressive Muscle Relaxation (tensing and releasing muscles quickly), Uttanasana (Standing Forward Bend), and Vrikshasana (Tree Pose).

- Reiki self-healing: As a Reiki master, I utilise Reiki immediately to restore balance. I also reach out to my Reiki mentor and batchmates via a WhatsApp group for urgent healing assistance if needed. Calling is always an option when required.

- Prepared support network: I keep a "3 AM friends list" ready, ensuring I have people who can offer support, motivation, or reach out to me urgently if needed.

- Healthcare professionals: I also keep the contact information of my doctors, therapists, and coaches well planned, like parachutes ready to help me land safely back on my feet.

- Consulting mentors: I reach out to my yoga therapist mentors when needed for guidance.

- Reiki, Angel therapy, and affirmations: I use Reiki and Angel therapy to instantly relax my nervous system, allowing me to be mindful before doing anything else.

Additionally, I use Louise Hay's affirmations in the following way:-

- Bless the situation (three times): No matter how difficult, evil, or terrifying it seems.
- Thank the situation (three times): Again, regardless of how challenging it may appear.

- Affirmations by Louise Hay-

"All is well. Everything is working out for my highest good.

Only good will come out of this situation, I am safe."

Practice and belief: As Louise Hay says, and with my experience since 2018, I've learned that no matter how harsh or dangerous the situation, it will always pass smoothly in a way that favours me.

### C) Self-Care- Extremely busy

"In August 2024, my superwoman syndrome became overactive. Along with my family, professional commitments, and weekly yoga sadhana and class-dance sessions, I started learning two new healing modalities from Monday to Saturday, and I began working on this book-writing project. For two months, each task was completed on time and vigorously.

After two and a half months, my energy—both mental and physical—began to deplete. Yet, I still pushed myself to complete each commitment daily."

*>>RESULT?*

By the end of October, my mind and body went on strike, and everything stood still, except, of course, my family and job commitments.

This brutal hit affected my brain and caused weakness in my eyelid muscles. Even after 5 months, I'm still recovering from this.

*>>REASON?*

I ignored daily physical activity like yoga, walking, aerobics, dance practice, or time spent with plants. I neglected to hydrate myself properly (as I started drinking more tea and coffee to work late) and had inadequate dinners.

Being constantly on the go and not achieving the results I expected led to stress, which wore my body down. My mind and body weren't getting enough oxygen due to the lack of physical activity and meditation. Dehydration prevented toxins, caused by stress, from flushing out, leading to brain fog, headaches, anxiety, and stomach infections.

>> *LESSONS I LEARNED:*

- Don't abandon yourself. If you leave yourself, don't expect others to take care of you. You must be the first one to support yourself with love and utmost care, listening to your inner voice and acknowledging the pain of your mind and body.
- Practicing self-care is especially important for extremely busy people. It supplies your mind and body with the essential air and water to work enthusiastically, maintaining optimal mental, emotional, and physical health.
- Only the practice of self-care helps not just to survive, but to thrive.
- Abandoning myself by sacrificing my self-care led to severe illness and high medical bills.

*My tips for self-care for the bustling community:-*
Instead of torturing your mind and body cruelly, pushing yourself to a breaking point, reflect on your inner turmoil and its root cause as soon as possible. Ignoring it will only extend the recovery time (sometimes for years).

- Any physical activity, even for just 5-7 minutes, is effective in helping your brain recalibrate.

- Meditation for 5-7 minutes (to invite oxygen with every breath and realign the mind and body).
- Perform 10 cycles of breathing in through the nose and exhaling through the mouth (this will reset your nervous system).
- Perform 10 cycles of breathing in through the left nostril and exhaling through the left nostril, while using your right thumb to block the right nostril. Tapping the left armpit will instantly release anxiety and normalise your breath.
- Regardless of the situation, continue to hydrate yourself.
- Listen to any genre of music you enjoy or read 1-2 pages of a fascinating book to break the cycle of anxiety, headaches, burnout, and other related issues.
- Choose your favourite 5–10-minute self-care activities that you can do daily to uplift your mood. Integrating easy self-care practices makes life more sustainable.

**"Small steps always make a huge difference."**___ Unknown

Anything worth having takes time.
One step at a time; You will get
there.

# CHAPTER FOURTEEN

# Chapter 13: Self-Care Plan

**"Carving your own path gets you to greatness quicker than following someone else's trail."**

(source: Google)

You belong to the Busy or Not-So-Busy Community (which is almost impossible nowadays)?

Still, everyone must choose 5–10-minute activities to take care of themselves that fit their conditions, convenience, and comfort.

### A) Daily Self-Care Plan

Select and plan activities that suit your comfort, convenience, and time constraints. Here are a few self-care ideas:-

### >> Gratitude Walk

- You can choose from a brisk walk, a regular walk, or a nature walk.
- Observe the surroundings, from the most minor details to the broader view.
- Be grateful for everything, from your body parts to the world around you (Air, water, earth, etc.).

- Even at your workplace, while going to and coming back from the washroom, keep saying "thank you, thank you..."
- While cooking, show gratitude for everything you touch and use.
- If, for any reason, you cannot leave the house, while moving around indoors, at each step, say "thank you, thank you, thank you" and keep repeating it (without any specific focus).

## >> *Meditation*

(Choose from any of the following or your method, and in this meditative state, listen to

your body's voice.)

- Observe your breath as it goes in and out (3-5 minutes).
- Play subliminal meditation music and sit for 5 minutes (you can gradually increase the duration).
- 5-minute guided meditation from YouTube.
- Just sit, write "RELAX" on a paper, observe it clearly, close your eyes, and visualise "RELAX" with closed eyes. Now, count backwards from 20 to 1, and on each count, repeat "RELAX" (repeat this from head to toe). When you reach 1, repeat "My whole body is relaxed" (3 times). Take three relaxed breaths and exit meditation.
- While walking to your work area, observe the movement of your body parts.
- Close your eyes, breathe in (3 times) through the nose, and on each inhale, affirm: "With this breath, I invite the universe in me." Exhale through the nose. Then, focus on the centre of your eyebrows and chant the name of the supreme power (as per your belief) on each breath-in and breath-out.

- While washing your hands or bathing, feel the temperature of the water on your hands and the movement of your hands as you do so.
- Before bathing, look into the water, thank it for cleansing you, and visualise/feel that with each drop of water, golden dust of the universe's blessings is showering on you, rejuvenating you.
- Whenever you want to come out of meditation:

    *Rub your hands together, cup your eyes, and look into your palms with a gentle smile. Bless yourself and your day.

    *Place your hands on your head, hug yourself with a smile and immense love, and slide your hands down your body with happy, loving energy.

    *Always offer thanks and gratitude to the universe for the opportunity and guidance, and to your mind-body for helping you calm down.

## >> *Breathing Work (May choose any one from the following)*

- A few rounds of breathing in through the nose and out through the mouth (keep alternating the speed of the breath, i.e., normal, fast, slow) and at the end (when comfortable) breathe in and out through the nose. Just observe and feel the breath.
- Breathe in for four counts, hold the breath for four counts, and exhale for four counts (it can be 3-3-3/5-5-5/4-8-8).
- Breathe in, hold the breath, chant any mantra/god's name as per your belief/any affirmation like "I am happier/calm/relaxed," and breathe out.

- At the workplace or while working from home, breathe in (close eyes) and breathe out (open eyes) for 4-5 counts. It will relax your mind and eyes simultaneously.

>> *Quick Way to Cut the Loop of Negative Thoughts*
*** Situation:** You are being snubbed in front of outsiders/ in public by anyone (family member/ higher

authority at work), and you can't speak a single word against it. Helplessness and failure to defend/

support yourself would start a loop of self-abasing, resulting in severe headaches/anxiety.

***Practice:-**

- Take three breaths, usually.
- Breathe in, squeeze all muscles from head to toe, and very slowly release muscles and breathe out with the statement: "My whole body is relaxed." (Repeat for five such breath-ins and breath-outs).
- Begin intentionally breathing in and out through the left nostril without counting. (If you find it difficult, place your right thumb on your right nostril).
- Also, keep your right hand on the left armpit and tap it.

Your headache might force you to stop, and you might think it is not benefiting you, but have faith and continue doing it at frequent intervals, at your convenience.

When you feel slightly better, do it for a longer duration. Believe me, this breathing will bring you out of the loop eventually.

A still and peaceful mind will give you an idea to make you feel happier and loved.

>> *Logic of Left-Nostril Breathing*

- This is a yogic practice and also a scientific fact.
- Right-nostril breathing is linked with the sympathetic nervous system (responsible for the mind's fight or flight response), which triggers an arousal/active/ stressful state. You will feel heated air from the right nostril.
- Left-nostril breathing relates to the parasympathetic nervous system (responsible for the mind's rest and calmer response), creating a stress/anger-alleviating state. You will feel cool air from the left nostril.
- With focused left-nostril breathing, after a few breaths, you will begin to feel cool air entering and exiting. Even this cool air you might feel in your mouth and throat. Slowly, it will cool down your mind.

>> *Physical Movement*

(for duration as per your time constraints/health conditions)

- Yoga/aerobics
- favourite sport
- Stretch each body part
- Mind games (with children)
- Dance
- Combine stretches/yoga asanas with any song
- Reading/listening to motivational books (as small as 1 page daily)
- Connect with nature or your supreme power, as per your beliefs, and chant its name, or recite any mantra, religious scripture, or verse for mental strength and inner guidance.
- Connect with Mother Earth through plants, gardening, walking on grass, or walking barefoot in the garden.

* If, for any reason, you cannot move out into nature, consider growing plants at home. Water them daily and watch them grow. Whenever you have time, sit next to them and observe them closely; it will be a therapeutic experience for you.

* For fun, choose any intention, sit closely next to a plant, and say with excitement (as if it is done): "You know, I am so happy and grateful for ... (your intention) is done."

>> *Affirmations-*

Phrases that, when repeated regularly aloud, mentally, or in writing, change negative thoughts and behaviour patterns of you and your family.

Choose either one affirmation from the following sections or any two sections as per your choice and time constraints.

> *For Self (3x)* – Anyone in the beginning and later, as per your convenience:-

- "I am happy, I am healthy"
- "(Your name), I behold you with eyes of love and glory in your God-given abilities. You are a blessed child of God, and God loves you. Divine health, happiness ... manifest through (your name)."
- "I send myself the blessing that all the goodness that I desire comes into my life. Also, send me the blessing of health and well-being."
- "I am a magnet for success in everything I do."
- "I am the co-creator of my life."
- "I invite God with me in today's day to walk with me and work with me in his magical way."
- "I am a happy, healthy, peaceful, and loving child of God."

- "I love myself unconditionally the way I am, so I speak for my grace and express myself clearly."
- "I am always surrounded by happy, helping, kind, and loving people around me."
- "I always attract the right people and the right situations in my life to grow."
- "My income from my work is growing day by day in quantity. The more I receive, the more I give. The more I give, the more I receive."
- "I am a responsible, strong, loving, and capable child of God OR I am a responsible, strong, loving, and capable soul."
- "I have everything in all areas of my life to be whole and complete."
- "Whenever I have to pay my bills, I receive more than enough money in advance from unexpected sources."
- "I love money, money loves me."
- "The universe and I love each other's company; we are good friends. I love the universe, the universe loves me."
- "I love and respect my children, my children love and respect me."
- "I deserve happiness, love, and health to celebrate my life."

> *For Family*

- "Everywhere I and my family are taken care of by the Universe. My family and I are blessed children of God."
- "Only the best comes to me and my family."
- "I invite God to be with me and my family, walk at each step, and work with me and my family in his magical way. Also, surround me and my family in his protection."

- "I am so happy and thankful that an abundance of wonderful miracles of celebrations and financial blessings are overflowing in my life and my family's life."
- "I am so happy that my family and I are financially independent and happily earning more than enough in our professions."
- "My family and I are surrounded and highly respected by loving, kind, helping, and happier seniors, colleagues, and subordinates at our jobs."
- "My family and I's earnings help us to travel in and overseas anywhere in the world easily, smoothly, and in God's magical way."
- "My family and I are blessed more than enough and chosen to serve mankind in our capacity."
- "I send my family and me the blessing that all the goodness that we desire comes into our lives. Also send me and my family the blessings of health and well-being."

### > *For Food, Water, House, Earth, Vehicles*

- "My family and I live in a blessed, happy, peaceful, and loving house surrounded by clean air and healthy water."
- "Our house is blessed with a continuous supply of water and electricity."
- "My kitchen is full of eatables to feed and give us energy."
- "My family and I are blessed and sustained by Mother Earth."
- "My family and I are blessed with high-quality vehicles to help us commute easily."

>> *Gratitude-*

To Count the Blessings You and Your Family Are Enjoying

i)Time- In the morning, evening, or night, as per your convenience.

ii) Where- Keep one separate notebook (called a journal) to jot down the gratitude.

- If you are a homemaker, do gratitude any time.
- If you are a professional (online or offline), try to do it before going to sleep. Otherwise, do it at your convenient time.

iii) How- In writing or mentally.

*I prefer to express gratitude in writing because when it is done in writing, the mind keeps track of the blessings for which gratitude is expressed, and you believe that you area blessed person.

* For example:-

- "I am so happy and grateful for my comfortable house."
- "I am grateful for the loving bond between me and my family."
- "I am grateful for the farmers and the food we eat to sustain us."
- "I am so happy and grateful for the sun, moon, stars, sky, all weather, trees and earth in our life."
- "I am so happy and grateful that only the best comes to me and my family."
- "I am so happy and grateful for my house help and all modern electronic gadgets that make our life comfortable."

- "I am so happy and grateful for all the helpful, kind, and supportive people around us."
- "I am so happy and grateful for all the favours I get on shopping from shopkeepers/social sites."
- "I am so happy and grateful for the healthier cells, muscles, nerves, tissues, hormones, glands, hair strands, skin, nails, and blood's each drop from head to toe."
- "I am so happy and grateful for my family's spiritual bonding."
- "I am so happy and grateful for being a grateful person."

* Sometimes I do gratitude mentally or aloud:

- While applying body lotion and massaging my foot soles with ghee or coconut oil at night to relax them, I give thanks and bless each body part, saying, "I am so happy and grateful for..."
- Sometimes, while brushing my teeth in the morning or at night, I take a moment to be grateful for all my facial features.
- Sometimes I do gratitude in a meditative state. Before slipping into bed, I close my eyes and recollect:

#* Happy moments (all or at least 3 happy moments). I relive those moments, open my eyes, and
write them in my gratitude journal.

#* Any bad/unhappy moments at work/home, I relive those moments, feel them again. I open my
eyes and write the positive lessons (at least one or two) I learned from this situation, and write
gratitude: "I am so happy and grateful that I learned that...."

- In the beginning, your mind might find it difficult to see the positive side of any bad moment, but don't accept your mind's flight mode. Instead, think intentionally, give it time, and believe me, it will provide you with some positive lessons to feel better. Then pour it into your journal.
- If something grievous happened that hurt you deeply, and the intensity of the hurt is still alive, then make sure not to sleep at any cost on the bed of burning coal (i.e., hurt moments).
- Keep a separate journal (name it as the "Emotional Vomit Journal") and "vomit" your hurt feelings, name them, address them, your anger, cry (if you want to), and what you wanted to do in that situation.
- Think of any lesson learned or any decision made to stand for your respect/esteem in a better way.
- Hug yourself tightly across your shoulders and repeat: "(Your name), I love you unconditionally, no matter what" (until you feel better). Feel the love. Open your happy journal and write gratitude: "I am so happy and grateful for what I learned that…" (for the lesson you learned/decision made).

>> Why Gratitude?

- Gratitude makes us appreciate the value of something (e.g., air, water, electricity, home, health, freedom to breathe, etc.). We're less likely to take it for granted.
- With gratitude, we become greater participants in our lives rather than just being spectators or living in victim mode, grabbing any opportunity to find a shoulder to lean on and cry.

- Gratitude blocks negative and toxic emotions, substituting them with happy hormones and less anxiety/stress.
- A grateful disposition helps an individual cope with and recover from any trauma or adversity.
- One learns to accept life as it is and is grateful for the special blessings that come in the form of good things, good relationships, and good people around.

### >> Blessings

A blessing is an action of sending healing energy for divine protection, a favour (small to bigger) for the betterment of yourself, your family, friends, your talents, all natural elements , strangers, etc., from the heavens/supreme power.

During my search on "blessings and their root in our holy books" and the origin of the word "bless," I came across an article (writer unknown) that stated:

- Holy Bible's verse Numbers 6:24-26: "The Lord bless you and keep you; the Lord make his face shine on you and be gracious to you; the Lord turn his face toward you and give you peace."
- The Hebrew concept of "blessing" (barak) involves not only receiving favour from God but also becoming a channel through which others are blessed.

#### > My Daily Blessing Practice for Myself and My Family

- "Send me and my family the blessing that all the goodness that we desire comes into our lives. Also send the blessing of health and well-being."
- I practice blessing in various ways, e.g.

- Bless today's day (3x) with an abundance of happiness, success, and fulfilment.
- Bless my office (3x)/bless the children's study institution.
- Bless ... situation (3x), thank you ... situation (3x) – in any untoward situation.
- Bless you ... (3x), thank you ... (any of the following) (3x) for a favourable outcome of any event like:

  *. Any exam/interview,
  *. Operation/emergency,
  *. Meeting (official or any business deal),
  *. Special celebration (get-together/party),
  *. Traveling and your transport medium (flight/train/car or bus (of self/family's any member),
  etc.]


- Bless the gold or any other valuable item (3x), thank you ... item (3x) – if it is lost/you are not finding it as of now.
- Bless you (3x) with excellent health to live a happier life – to bless an unhealthy plant/animal/bird.
- Bless You (3x) – for anyone you see in trouble (accident/any other) while commuting on the road or any medium of transport.
- Bless you (3x) with a fast recovery. Thank you (3x). My family and I are healthy and safe. When we come across an ambulance, we are grateful.
- Bless the lift/escalator (3x), thank you lift/escalator (3x) – before entering into/stepping into the lift/escalator.
- Bless the traffic jam (3x), thank you for the traffic jam (3x) – if stuck in a traffic jam/getting late to reach somewhere.

- Bless the situation (3x), thank you situation (3x) – if you have heard/read about any calamity in any part of your country/the world.

> *Why Bless?*

Practising blessings in my daily life fills my day and my family's each day and each moment (in various ways) with confidence, happiness and ease.

It also works as a saviour in seen and unseen circumstances, overflowing divine magical blessings in our lives in incredible ways beyond imagination. Even the most difficult situations dissolve smoothly in favourable outcomes without hurting you, any family member, or anyone else for whom you send blessings.

Since 2015, this has been my daily ritual: to bless myself, my spouse, and my children daily (as explained above) for health, happiness, protection, success, my spouse's office and my children's studies and academic institutions.

In October 2022, it had been raining heavily since morning. My son and his friend went in the car to give their +2 pre-board exam. Around 3:30 PM, I called my son.

He said the heavy rain had flooded the roads, and cars were floating here and there in the water. With a thud, their car was caught in a whirl and began to twirl. Within minutes, the car filled with smoke. For a second, excessive coughing and suffocation tensed him and his friend.

Suddenly, they got an idea and gave the car a continuous boost, driving it out of the water. They then got out of the car, took the lift, and reached home.

I got goosebumps.

I was in tears with deep gratitude to the divine. While my husband and I were busy with our jobs, my daily blessings surrounded my son and his friend with an invisible protection shield, guiding them out, and ultimately saving two lives.

> *Logic of Practising Blessing*

The effort of repeating blessings daily and frequently allows our mind to shift into auto mode. When the mind enters auto mode, the unconscious mind begins to perform these actions naturally, just as it would with any other habit.

Your mind becomes attuned to bringing all magical incidents into your life, fostering a deeper connection to the divine or your higher self, which in turn keeps you content. This contentment boosts your mind and physical growth.

Others look up to you for support and inspiration to overcome challenges. You become a magnet for positive, safe, and happier outcomes in your life and the lives of those you care about.

**"The more you bless, the more blessings you receive. The more blessings you receive, the more you bless."**

**>> Cope up from any fearful situation/difficult person at home or in office work:**

*1)* Affirmation by Louise Hay, Works as a saviour no matter what:

- Bless the situation (3x)
- Thank the situation (3x)
- Affirm (3x) :
- "All is well, Everything is working out for (my) highest good,
- Out of this situation, only good will come, (I am) safe. "

In the above affirmation, "(my)" can be substituted with any desired outcome or any person's name. Similarly, "(I am)" would be substituted with specific intentions, as follows:-

**i) Situation** – My child is appearing for an interview or exam:

- Bless the situation (3x)
- Thank the situation (3x)
- Affirmation- "All is well, Everything is working out for (my) highest good, Out of this situation, only good will come, (I am) safe. " (3x)

**ii) Situation** – A friend is hurt or going through some health issue:

- Bless the situation (3x)
- Thank the situation (3x)
- "All is well, Everything is working out for (my) highest good, Out of this situation, only good will come, (I am) safe. " (3x)

**iii) Situation** – Your children are late to reach home from school, forgot or couldn't complete some vital paper for a meeting, or are stuck in traffic and are late for a meeting:

- Bless the situation (3x)
- Thank the situation (3x)
- "All is well, Everything is working out for (my) highest good, Out of this situation, only good will come, (I am) safe. " (3x)

**iv) Situation** – You came to know that someone might face strict action due to a mistake at work:

- Bless the situation (3x)
- Thank the situation (3x)
- "All is well, Everything is working out for (my) highest good, out of this situation, only good will come, (I am) safe. " (3x)"

**v) Situation** – A day is fixed for your get-together with friends, but it's on a working day, so you need to leave:

- Bless the situation (3x)
- Thank the situation (3x)
- "All is well, Everything is working out for (my) highest good, Out of this situation, only good will come, (I am) safe. " (3x)

**vi) Situation** – You wish for a party/high-level meeting you have to attend (as host or invitee) to be filled with magical moments:

- Bless the situation (or party/meeting) (3x)
- Thank the situation (or party/meeting) (3x)
- "All is well, Everything is working out for (my) highest good, Out of this situation, only good will come, (I am) safe. " (3x)

**$ NOTE**

- Repeat the above affirmation according to the gravity and longevity of the situation, until you feel mentally peaceful or until the desired outcome is achieved.
- This affirmation helps you to emerge from any unfavourable or difficult situation, provided your intention is honest, or if any wrong in your work was

unintentional and not meant to harm anyone.

- In any situation, this affirmation ensures that it will pass without harming you or the concerned party (whether it involves someone known or unknown to you).
- When you perform this affirmation for someone (known or unknown), your good deed will return blessings to you (or your family member) at any point in time, as every action has a corresponding reaction.
- When you perform this affirmation for someone (known or unknown), your good deed will return blessings to you (or your family member) at any point in time, as every action has a corresponding reaction.

***II) hurt with harsh words from a person:***
**i)** While taking a shower, wait for a second:

- Pray to God/universe/any other name as you know to charge each hydrogen atom/drop of water with its blessings/energy.
- When charged water falls on your body, feel golden dust (which represents universe blessings) falling on your head and washing away the words from your mind into the drainpipe.
- Open your eyes and see that the person who spoke harsh words to you is also being washed away into the pipe with the blessed water. Repeat it intentionally three to five times.
- Breathe in through your nose and breathe out through your mouth with the belief that you have freedom from the grip of pain and hurt thoughts.

**ii)** Affirm:

- "I bless you for the goodness of God that is within you."
- In our daily lives, we encounter many people—known, unknown, and strangers —both at home and outside, who behave or speak in ways that may hurt or insult us.
- They hardly care for our feelings.
- In these situations, avoid arguing or getting triggered. Instead, repeat the above affirmation, and it will immediately cool you down.
- With practice, your mind will begin to repeat this affirmation automatically, helping you feel better.

>Logic-

Why and how can I bless the person who insulted me? This question might pop up after reading this, right?

Your continuous criticism won't change his behaviour or thoughts—he is least concerned about your feelings.

Only you can feel your disturbed emotions. Therefore, you must prioritise your happiness and work on it.

Sometimes it happens to me also. My mind throws so many logical reasons not to bless the harsh person, but I convince it with the smart logic that, "Yes! I felt bad and wanted to raise my voice. This person wants to make me feel sad or insulted, but I will do what I want. No one can rule over me. Blessings sent to him will return to me only to make me a happier person."

***III) Smartly Deal with a Difficult Person:***

Way back in 2015, I read an affirmation (writer unknown) on Google:

***"Sending you the blessing that all the goodness and success that you desire come into your life. Also send you the blessings of health and well-being."***

(It was mentioned that it would either change the difficult person's behaviour or the person would move away from your life, provided you don't think or speak any bad or curse words to him.)

Since then, I have been using this affirmation and enjoying its benefits as needed.

At the workplace, whenever I use this affirmation, either the XYZ person is transferred or their behaviour turns softer, or I am transferred to another branch.

At home, where moving away from a difficult person is impossible, whenever I use this affirmation:-

>* If the person is an own family member, either that person gets busy with their own

work in such a way that their focus and behaviour change toward me, or

situations change in my favour, or the person's behaviour starts changing slowly.

>* If the person is an extended family member, either XYZ person will move away

from you, surprisingly, in a cordial way, or the person's interference in your life

would slowly diminish and eventually stop forever.

*$ Note:*

In the beginning, even when reading the above affirmation, your logical mind might rebel against it.

You might think, "How can I bless this XYZ person, whose desire comes into his life when he is disturbing me/ hurting me so much?"

Believe me, if you speak this affirmation consistently to the difficult person, even if you are just saying it for the sake of it, and not from the heart, despite your angry thoughts, it will work in your favour magically.

*IV) yoga asanas* - to release stress/worries faster
*i) Legs up the wall pose (viprit karni pose)-*
>steps-

- Place your yoga mat next to a wall with lots of open space.
- Sit next to the wall with your right hip pressing against it and your knees bent with your feet on the floor.
- Place your hands behind your hips and lean your weight into them to lift your feet off the floor.
- Turn your hips to face the wall and lift your legs up on it to rest against it.
- Release the weight of your torso onto the floor and relax.
- Place your hands in a comfortable position and gently lower the weight of your legs toward the floor.
- Hold for as long as you'd like, gently focusing on your breath and slowing its rhythm as you allow gravity to assist venous return.

ii) One-legged Seated Forward bend (Janu shirshasana)
>Steps-

- Extend your legs in front of you, toes flexed, quadriceps contracted.
- Bend your right knee, placing your right foot against your inner left thigh and your right heel close to your perineum.
- Now, breathe in, raise both your arms over your head, and lengthen your spine.
- Exhale, and slowly from your back, contract your belly, core, and reach with your arms to grasp the centre of the hamstring muscles. Be gentle with the forward bend. Stop where your body doesn't allow.
- After counting 5 seconds, inhale and slowly come up.
- Repeat the same on the left side.

iii) Child pose (balasana)
> Steps

- Sit back on your heels by bending your knees and feet towards your hips.
- Extend the knees distance equal to the mat width.
- Exhale and slowly bend forward, extending your arms in front of you. Allow your forehead to rest on the mat.
- Let your entire body relax. Focus on your breath, taking deep, even breaths. Stay in this position for 1-2 minutes or as long as comfortable.
- Exhale and gently lift your torso, then return to a kneeling position.

iv) Happy baby pose (Anand bal asana)
>Steps-

- Lie down on your back.
- Stretch out your legs and arms, bring your breath back to normal through deep breathing, and stay here for about 6 breaths.
- Inhale and bend your knees, placing your feet close to your buttocks with hip-distance apart. Exhale completely here.
- Inhale and raise your feet from the floor, bringing the soles facing upwards towards the ceiling. With your hands, hold onto your feet, pressing the soles slightly towards the floor with your elbows.
- Taking a deep breath, gently press the feet and knees downwards while pulling the abdomen in, tightening the muscles around the area.
- Maintain the posture for five breaths.

- Gently release the hands and bring the legs dow,n and place them on the floor with the legs stretched out and relax completely here.

v) Corpse pose (Shavasana)

One of my favourites that help restore my calmness as quickly as possible are Viprit Karni and Anand Bal Asana (where I always see my childhood image playing, laughing, and dancing).

If you're new to yoga or completely unaware of it, then it's best to start with Corpse Pose.

> Steps-

- Lie down, close your eyes.
- Chin and nose toward the ceiling, toes falling outside naturally, palms facing the ceiling, and arms slightly away from the body.
- Take 3 breaths, feeling the temperature of the air beneath both nostrils. (5 counts)
- Breathe in, tighten all the muscles from head to toe, including your fingers, for 3 counts. Breathe out, and release each muscle very slowly.
- After the 3 breaths, take one more deep breath in, tighten all the muscles, hold the breath for 3 counts, and very slowly release each muscle while exhaling.
- Drop your whole body weight on the place where you are lying.
- Now that your mind and body are relaxed, keep your eyes closed and be in this stillness for as long as you feel comfortable. (If you prefer, play flute music, the sound of water, or any relaxing subliminal at a very low volume in the beginning.)

- In the stillness, keep your eyes closed and focus on the music.
- As you feel good, inhale and, while exhaling, turn to the right side with the support of your left hand.
- While on your side, breathe in, exhale, and keeping your eyes closed, sit up. Rub your hands, cup your eyes.
- Look into your palms with a gentle smile and say: "I am happy, I am healthy."
- Keeping the smile on your face, place both hands, one over the other, on your heart. Feel your heartbeat and be grateful that you are alive. Repeat: "I am happy, I am healthy."
- Keeping the smile on your face, hug yourself with immense love across your shoulders. Repeat: "(Your name), I am happy, I am healthy."
- Now, transfer your love-filled energy by sliding your hands over each body part and keep repeating with a smile: "I am happy, I am healthy."

*B) On Weekends/Holidays/Leaves/Vacations:*

i) Count and write the blessings you are blessed with through various privileges in different levels of life.

ii) Intentionally spend your day to BLESS

- Yourself, your family, for health (of each cell, muscle, nerve, tissue, gland, hormone, organ, and body part) Professional well-being, happiness.
- Your house (house safety, sun/moon/sky visibility).
- Water, electricity, bed, plants in your house, greenery around you.
- Vehicles, a variety of clothes, and the internet.
- House help or any service provider (e.g., doctor).
- Facilities available near your house.

- Past moments that still make you feel happier.
- Health, happiness, and well-being of your parents, siblings, their children, friends, neighbours, staff/officers, colleagues, drivers who help you commute, guards in your locality.
- The world, the earth, the environment.
- Your and your family's talents.
- Your kitchen provides you with everything to fuel energy in you and your family.
- Your job/business, work, workplace.
- Your new learnings, mentors.

With practice, new ideas for blessings will automatically come to you.

On my days off from the office, I do blessings in detail through meditations and while moving from place to place throughout the day.

iii) Meditate for a longer time

- If you are a beginner or want to experience it, breathe in (observe the movement of air entering through your nostrils) and breathe out (observe the movement of air exiting through your nostrils) for at least 5-7 minutes.
- If you are a practitioner for some time, intentionally feel oxygen going into each organ for at least 20 minutes.
- Look at the sky, observe its colour, clouds, birds flying, its vastness, its peace. Close your eyes and feel it within you. Open your eyes and repeat the practice for at least 10-20 minutes.
- Go to the park, sit on the grass barefoot (if you want, you can use a mat to sit). Feel the grass, its texture, the noises around you, the rustling of leaves. Feel the air on your face, breathe in the fragrance of the sand/flowers

around you. Breathe out all unnecessary thoughts. Feel the love of Mother Earth that sustains us.

iv) Reflect your growth in:

- Relationships (self, family, friends, social, environmental)
- Health (physical exercise, diet)
- Finance (graph of earnings, spending, savings, investments)
- Profession (career)
- Spiritual (connection with self, your mind, emotional and physical state, and your higher self)

>With self-reflections, I could upgrade and uplift myself bit by bit but consistently since 2015 at my own pace, resulting in:

- A better sense of self
- Better relationships
- Stronger decision-making
- Increased confidence
- Enhanced problem-solving state of mind
- Emotional intelligence
- A carved niche of satisfactory growth

>However, reflection makes me wiser and strong enough to prioritise self-care, which involves accepting disturbances, practising self-talk through positive affirmations (as shared above), and employing other healing techniques (as described above) to clear brain fog and break the loop of negative thoughts.

>This aligns my mind and body to provide clarity and ideas that enable me to bounce back as smoothly as possible.

> How I do self-reflection:-

** Journaling:

- I reflect on my growth, particularly during challenging times. I try to be gentle with myself, take responsibility for my mistakes (if any), without judgment or self-abasement, and learn from them or challenging situations. I explore my triggers, examining what, how, why, and when they occur.

** Meditations & Breathing Techniques:

- These are my tools for staying grounded and reflecting deeply on my thoughts, actions, and emotional states.

** New Learning:

- If necessary, I embark on a new learning journey to upgrade or enhance myself, ensuring continuous growth.

** Gratitude:

- I celebrate my wins, no matter how small, and use gratitude as a tool to break the negativity loop in my mind.

**Connecting with Nature:

- Nature helps me recalibrate. I take time to observe the world around me and reconnect with its beauty and tranquillity.

** Set Small, Specific Goals:

- When necessary, I set clear and attainable goals, ensuring I focus on meaningful actions rather than the time spent.

** Focus on Generative Moments:

- Instead of chasing time lengths or ticking off to-do lists, I focus on the quality of the moments and the energy they generate.

** Reading Books:

- Books offer me new perspectives and wisdom that enhance my self-reflection process.

** Connecting with My Inner Child:

- I frequently check in with my inner child, ensuring that he/she is happy and calm. I sit with my crayons, brush pens, and glitter colours to:
- Express gratitude by drawing an image and writing positive affirmations artistically on a sheet, which I then place on the wall in front of me.

* Sometimes, I draw landscapes, sunflowers, mangoes-simple things I used to draw as a child. This
instantly fills me with immense joy.

* If I'm feeling low, hurt, or tense, I close my eyes, rewind the emotions of a specific situation, and

in the present moment, I doodle or draw lines, "vomiting" all anger and frustration. This helps to

wash away the inner turmoil through tears.

* After emptying myself emotionally, I lie down in Shavasana (corpse pose) and take deep breaths

to relax the tension in both my mind and body.

* Using bright colours, I sometimes use my non-dominant hand to draw or write about my

emotions.


- Under the guidance of an ICH-certified coach, Ms. Tapaswinee Hota Choudhary, I learnt to connect with my Inner child on a deeper level and became a certified Inner Child Healing (ICH) Practitioner.

* I have a better idea to stay connected to my inner child

* I am equipped with quick fix healing techniques in the context of nowadays busy

life's mood swings

* Still I dance on life's tunes (unexpected twists and turns in any direction) yet on

My Steps.


> Laughter Yoga:


- I imagine my inner child sitting in front of me, holding her soft hands, kissing her from a few inches away, and laughing loudly (3 times).
- This exercise fills me with pure, innocent love and instantly eases the tensed muscles, especially during adverse situations.

These self-care techniques, when practised consistently, work like spirals that gradually heal your spiritual, emotional, mental, physical, social, and professional health, simply by paying attention to your thoughts and feelings.

As I once heard, life first gives you a surprise test (a challenge), and by the time you're ready to answer (by adapting to the changed circumstances), it changes the question (a new challenge of a different level).

With various self-care techniques, your small victories will accumulate, building confidence in you to tackle life's challenges with perseverance. I express my deep gratitude to Atomic Habits (by James Clear) for transforming my life by teaching me the "Two-Minute Rule", to build a new habit muscle by starting with the smallest action for at least 2 minutes daily.

" Until July 2024, I was practising my self-Yoga Sadhana through Bodhi School of Yoga's online sessions. However, in August 2024, I fell ill with a stomach infection, which took a week to recover from.

By the end of September 2024, one of my co-practitioners reached out, reminding me that I had skipped Yoga for almost two months.

That realisation left me feeling guilty, and despite my best intentions, I couldn't return to the mat.

Even the arrival of the New Year 2025 couldn't motivate me enough to step on my mat.

However, when I encountered Atomic Habits, I found myself caught in a loop of self-blame and guilt, surrounded by daily commitments.

The two-minute rule from the book gave me the breakthrough I needed.

The next day, I got on the mat and did stretching for just 2 minutes. I continued with this for a week, and the following week, I was practising Yoga for 10 minutes without effort.In February 2025, I joined an online Yoga Sadhana with the excellent teacher, Ms. Shweta (also a Bodhi student), and I'm now thoroughly enjoying Yoga again."

Now, I'm applying the two-minute rule to strengthen my self-care muscles in various ways:

- Practising daily gratitude, blessings, and affirmations
- Continuing my Yoga practice and learning different healing techniques to be of more use to myself and others
- Exploring new self-care learning techniques like scripting emotions and colour therapy
- Reaching out to my neighbours, friends, parents, and relatives to build my communication muscle (something I had previously resisted)

> I practice self-care not just to survive but to thrive.

- It is now essentially a daily part of my routine.
- I have learned the hard way that it takes a long time for me to recover when I don't take care of myself.

> While learning and applying these techniques, it's important to remember:-

- Life's first principle is 'to move,' and it always ensures that it sticks to it in any case.
- Sometimes it offers smooth, buttery rides, and sometimes spiky ones as well.
- There will be speed bumps, and they can either make you or break you.

- During these speed bumps (such as sickness, busy schedules, travel, or family rituals), it's better to slow down rather than completely stop the car (i.e., miss self-care practices for two consecutive days), as it breaks the momentum.
- Once you stop, you may find yourself in the "out of sight, out of mind" phase.
- But no matter how high the speed bump, the solution to bouncing back is always self-care.

> Self-care isn't magic per se, but it surely works like a magic wand if done consistently, mindfully, intentionally, and systematically.
> With slow and steady self-care, you will:-

- Become an observer, rather than an absorber.
- Step up to become an inspiration to others.
- Finally, transform into the designer and creator of your world, rather than merely a consumer of what the world offers you.

As the saying goes, ***"A desert cannot quench your thirst."*** This perfectly applies to our lives. Be the change and bring about the change with self-care.

# Transformation with Self-Care

(source: Canva)

"Your transformation represents more than what is just skin deep; it represents your motivation, drive, and willingness to constantly improve."

(source- Jinder Mahal - selffa.com-Google)

# Fun Activity For Self-Care

1)

# Choose 3 Words for Today

Daily Positivity +

```
M  J  R  S  T  V  U  R  O  Z
E  W  S  U  C  C  E  S  S  A
N  I  A  B  Q  G  H  L  W  P
E  T  V  X  B  A  I  S  C  A
R  A  Q  W  A  Y  Y  C  O  T
G  W  E  A  L  T  H  J  M  I
Y  G  A  Q  A  O  G  K  F  E
K  I  N  D  N  E  S  S  O  N
C  A  N  I  C  Q  X  V  R  C
P  R  A  W  E  J  T  U  T  E
```

Let the 3 words you choose be with you today.

2) Journalling Prompts-

# Productive Journaling Prompts

Write down 3 simple goals you want to achieve today.

Write down something you want to let go of today.

Write down one challenge you will take on today.

Write down a daily affirmation for success.

Write down a routine that is important to you.

Write down something you are proud of yourself for.

3) Count your gratitudes creatively-
>>Steps-

- Sit in a comfortable place.
- Collect yours or your children's pencil or plastic crayons.
- Fill the flower with your favourite colours
- Now, write the words of gratitude in each petal.

4) Challenge Yourself, Change Your Mind- Write with Non-Dominant Hand

>>Steps-

- When under stress or mentally confused, do this exercise
- Take colours, colored pen, write anything you want with your non-dominant hand
- Non-dominant hand means the hand that you don't use to write or to do work.
- As you'll write slowly, your mind will also slow down, bringing you fear or anxiety.